Home-School Learning Resources

Every purchase of a Facet book helps to fund CILIP's advocacy, awareness and accreditation programmes for information professionals.

Home-School Learning Resources

A Guide for Home-Educators, Teachers, Parents and Librarians

Christinea Donnelly

facet publishing

Published by Facet Publishing
7 Ridgmount Street, London WC1E 7AE
www.facetpublishing.co.uk

Facet Publishing is wholly owned by CILIP: the Library and Information Association.

British Library Cataloguing in Publication Data
A catalogue record for this book is available from the British Library.

ISBN 978-1-78330-490-5 (paperback)
ISBN 978-1-78330-491-2 (PDF)
ISBN 978-1-78330-544-5 (EPUB)

First published 2021

Text printed on FSC accredited material.

MIX
Paper from responsible sources
FSC® C013604
FSC www.fsc.org

Typeset from author's files in 10/13 pt University Oldstyle and Expressway by Flagholme Publishing Services.
Printed and made in Great Britain by CPI Group (UK) Ltd, Croydon, CR0 4YY.

Beatus doctrina!

Contents

Introduction

The idea behind this book is a simple one: to point parents, teachers, educators, children and young people to excellent learning resources that will enrich knowledge, critical thinking and understanding of key subjects children are currently learning at school or from home. The book is arranged alphabetically by subject and is suitable for 4 to 16 years old. It is hoped such a guide will aid navigation through the myriad of information available online, offering an alternative to searching via Google or using Wikipedia.

This book is about finding different methods of learning through activities, hands-on experiments and crafts or using archival materials, images and documents. It is about tapping into the wealth of information that experts, academics and curators have packaged and designed to support the next generation of scientists, teachers, writers, historians and curious minds. Their enthusiasm can be infectious and their materials inspiring. There are certainly lots of lesson plans and classroom presentations included, not just for use by teachers but for parents and educators too. They provide structure to subjects or topics, offering work plans and information as well as providing links with the curriculum. It can be so easy to miss these resources as it takes time to locate and evaluate them and that is a commodity many teachers, parents or educators often have in short supply. They have been researched and evaluated from hundreds of online sources that include museums, universities, libraries, charities and interest bodies from around the UK. Having a guide that takes the user directly to these rich sources may well help, not only with learning, but also by bringing some fun into that learning too.

Why is access to such resources needed?

The unprecedented closure of schools during 2020/2021, due to the COVID-19 pandemic, left many children and young people learning online from home, supported by bewildered and often unprepared parents. The publication *Coronavirus and Home Schooling in Great Britain: April to June 2020 – Analysis of Home Schooling in Great Britain During the Coronavirus (COVID-19) Pandemic* (Opinions and Lifestyle Survey, 22 July 2020, www.ons.gov.uk/peoplepopulationandcommunity/educationandchildcare/articles/coronavirusandhomeschoolingingreatbritain/apriltojune2020) found that in addition to children using the digital resources provided by their schools and accessed via online learning platforms, 55% had used digital online learning resources found by a parent for a child aged 5–10 years. Equally so, 30% said they had used digital online learning resources found by a parent for a child aged 11–15 years and 24% used digital online learning resources found by a parent for a child aged 16–18 years. Excellent, free and accessible learning resources have never been more needed.

Since writing *Know It All, Find It Fast for Youth Librarians and Teachers* (2011, Facet Publishing) there has been a significant growth in the availability of online resources for learning and information. Those organisations who realised the online potential back in 2011 have been joined by a proliferation of groups, charities, museums, libraries and many more, all keen to package their information and resources into online educational tools for use by schools, teachers, parents and, most importantly, children and young people. This growth in availability has fortunately correlated to the development of quality, creativity and accessibility. The production of lesson plans by international charities on current topics, downloadable activities from scientific bodies and digitised paintings from art galleries, provide expert information, access to material that previously would have been difficult to find or use and bring subjects to life. The curriculum has become connected to the world outside the classroom.

There have been other growth areas too. Home education through choice has risen sharply with over 60,000 children reportedly being home-schooled according to official figures published by the UK Government's school admissions watchdog for 2018/2019. Clearly, some parents and carers are thinking differently about education and learning.

However, although elective home education may be increasing, the vast majority of children are still educated within our schools. Here too there has been a change in the materials and resources used to deliver lessons. Teachers now use a wide range of online interactive information resources with school children and young people accessing online learning platforms.

Hopefully, this guide can support parents, teachers, educators, children and young people to utilise materials that complement those offered by school, assist those educating children at home to discover new resources and promote the enjoyment of holistic learning to all.

How to use this book

The book is arranged alphabetically - why make it complicated? It covers the school curriculum subjects (identified in the text by [C]) and it covers popular topics children and young people either enjoy, such as Dinosaurs, or need to know about, such as Relationships and Sex, or offer learning experiences outside of the classroom, such as Nature. There is no claim to be comprehensive, that is not the intention, but it does offer an extensive collection of quality resources from hundreds of different organisations including museums, universities, libraries, charities and interest bodies from around the UK. Over 300 are included but almost double that number were researched. This was not about quantity but undoubtedly about quality. All the resources included have been selected because they are very good or excellent. If a resource warrants being highlighted as excellent, this has been indicated. It also includes some great web platforms that offer information, worksheets and interactive activities and these too were given the same scrutiny. And of course, it was important to find free resources that could be accessed easily. This was not about paid subscriptions to online services, which, of course, have their place and are important too.

Within some subject headings there are 'See also' references where appropriate. For example, those interested in Animals and Birds are likely to find material of interest within Nature. Or the curriculum subject PSHE (Personal, Social, Health and Economic Education), which covers learning about drugs, alcohol, online safety and health issues along with social skills and much more. Instead of including all those resources within PSHE, it was felt these would be better listed individually and those with a particular interest in PSHE encouraged to cross-reference to each specific topic.

There is an alphabetical index to search for specific terms that may span several fields of study. For example, there is certainly crossover with topics within History and Citizenship such as Black History and the Civil Rights Movement or Women's Suffrage and Voting Rights. There will be many more.

All the website addresses given have been checked and were correct at the time of going to press.

The National Curriculum

How you use this book will depend on whether you are a parent, educator or a teacher. For teachers, you may be looking for new resources for a familiar subject, or as an educator or parent, you may need materials to support home learning. Materials that bring learning to life. Firstly, there is nothing stopping you just diving into the alphabetical list (I would) but if you prefer a more considered approach there are some guiding resources below.

Equipping yourself with what your child is likely to study for each subject is essential. For this the Oak National Academy (https://teachers.thenational.academy) has the most accessible, easy to use and understandable curriculum for each subject. You can browse by subject or by key stage. In addition, it includes the following specialist lessons: Communication and Language; Creative Arts; Early Development and Learning; Independent Living; Numeracy; Physical Development and Therapies. It is an excellent resource and would be a suitable starting point for anyone embarking on home learning.

If your child is at school, you may want to understand what your child is being taught in the classroom. For a detailed overview of the National Curriculum visit: www.gov.uk/national-curriculum. It is important to realise that the school curriculum includes both the National Curriculum and religious and sex education. The National Curriculum is defined as a set of subjects and standards used within both primary and secondary schools with the aim that all children learn the same things. However, academies and independent schools do not have to follow the National Curriculum. For academies, the aim is to teach 'a broad and balanced' curriculum including English, Maths and Science, along with Religious Education. It is also important to realise that the National Curriculum has variations across the four nations - England, Northern Ireland, Scotland and Wales. These will be covered below.

National Curriculum in England

For the National Curriculum in England, children are organised into the following key stages, i.e., year groups, with an end of year assessment by the teacher.

Table taken from www.gov.uk/national-curriculum

Child's age	Year	Key stage	Assessment
3 to 4		Early Years	
4 to 5	Reception	Early Years	Teacher assessments (there's also an optional assessment at the start of the year)
5 to 6	Year 1	KS1	Phonics screening check
6 to 7	Year 2	KS1	National tests and teacher assessments in English, Maths and Science
7 to 8	Year 3	KS2	
8 to 9	Year 4	KS2	
9 to 10	Year 5	KS2	
10 to 11	Year 6	KS2	National tests and teacher assessments in English and Maths, and teacher assessments in Science
11 to 12	Year 7	KS3	
12 to 13	Year 8	KS3	
13 to 14	Year 9	KS3	
14 to 15	Year 10	KS4	Some children take GCSEs
15 to 16	Year 11	KS4	Most children take GCSEs or other national assessments

To find what is included in the curriculum by key stages and the programmes of study for each subject, visit: www.gov.uk/government/collections/national-curriculum.

Curriculum for Northern Ireland

The Curriculum for Northern Ireland applies to all 12 years of compulsory education. The current primary curriculum includes a Foundation Stage, which covers P1 and P2 (Years 1 and 2). Key Stage 1 covers P3 and P4 (Years 3 and 4) and Key Stage 2 covers P5, P6 and P7 (Years 5, 6 and 7). At post-primary level, Key Stage 3 covers Years 8, 9 and 10 and Key Stage 4 covers Years 11 and 12.

The current primary curriculum is made up of Religious Education (RE) and the following areas of learning: Language and Literacy; Mathematics and Numeracy; Arts; The World Around Us; Personal Development and Mutual Understanding; and Physical Education (PE).

The current post-primary curriculum includes Learning for Life and Work, which is made up of employability, personal development, local and global citizenship and home economics (at Key Stage 3). The post-primary curriculum also includes

Religious Education (RE) and the following areas of learning: Language and Literacy; Mathematics and Numeracy; Modern Languages; Arts; Environment and Society; Physical Education (PE); and Science and Technology. At Key Stage 4, the statutory requirements are Learning for Life and Work, Physical Education (PE), Religious Education (RE) and developing skills and capabilities.

For more information on the curriculum and programmes of learning visit: www.education-ni.gov.uk/articles/statutory-curriculum

Curriculum for Excellence in Scotland

The Curriculum for Excellence is Scotland's curriculum for children and young people aged 3-18 years.

There are excellent Nutshell guides for parents for the Curriculum for Excellence, which covers the broad general education from 3 to 14 years (ELC, P1-P7 and S1-S3) and the senior phase for ages 14-17 years (S4-S6). The senior phase is when young people take qualifications and courses to suit abilities and interests. For either Nutshell guide, visit: www.education.gov.scot/parentzone/learning-in-scotland/about-the-3-18-curriculum.

Within the Curriculum for Excellence in Scotland there are five curriculum levels within the broad general education for children and young people before they progress to the senior phase.

Within the curriculum levels, the year groups for the broad general education are ELC (3 to 5 years); P1 (4½ to 5½ years); P2 (6 years); P3 (7 years); P4 (8 years); P5 (9 years); P6 (10 years); and P7 (11 to 12 years). Within the senior phase, the year groups are S1 (13 years), S2 (14 years), S3 (15 years), S4 (16 years and National 5s), S5 (17 years and Scottish Highers) and S6 (18 years and Scottish Advanced Highers). Years S1 to S4 are mandatory; S5 to S6 are optional.

Table taken from www.education.gov.scot/parentzone/learning-in-scotland/broad-general-education

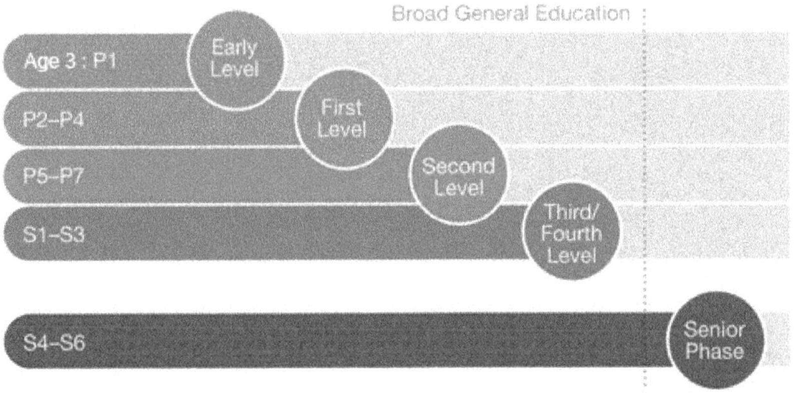

There are eight curriculum areas of learning and these are: Expressive Arts; Languages; Religious and Moral Education; Sciences; STEM; Health and Well-Being; Mathematics and Numeracy; Social Studies; and Technologies.

For more information about the key areas of learning within each curriculum level, visit: www.education.gov.scot/parentzone/learning-in-scotland/broad-general-education.

Curriculum in Wales

For an overview of the curriculum in Wales, visit: https://hwb.gov.wales. There are guidance documents available to download at: https://hwb.gov.wales/curriculum-for-wales-2008.

The curriculum in Wales is implementing some changes over the next year and there are some excellent guides available to download to explain the changes. For *A New Curriculum in Wales: A Guide for Children, Young People and Families*, visit: https://hwb.gov.wales/curriculum-for-wales/a-new-curriculum-in-wales-a-guide-for-children-young-people-and-families.

Or you can use the commendable easy read publication *A New Curriculum in Wales: Changing the Way Children and Young People Learn in School* https://hwb.gov.wales/curriculum-for-wales/a-new-curriculum-in-wales-easy-read.

For more information about the key areas of learning: Expressive Arts; Health and Well-being; Humanities; Languages, Literacy and Communication; Mathematics and Numeracy; and Science and Technology, visit: https://hwb.gov.wales/curriculum-for-wales.

Home education

Home education is the term used to describe the practice by which parents or carers decide to educate their children outside of the school system.

> 'The parent of every child of compulsory school age shall cause him to receive efficient full-time education ... either by regular attendance at school or otherwise.'
>
> Education Act 1996, section 7

That is, education is compulsory, schooling is not. Home education is different from home schooling or home learning through school closure, with parents electing to ensure that they will provide full-time education to their child. This does not require following the National Curriculum.

For those considering elective home education, there is guidance available. The guidance from the government in England called *Educating Your Child at Home* is available at: www.gov.uk/home-education. In addition, there is a further document - *Elective Home Education: Guidance for Parents* - available at: www.gov.uk/government/publications/elective-home-education.

Scotland's national home education support charity, Schoolhouse (www.schoolhouse.org.uk), offers information, support and advice, as well as links to a range of educational resources. It also has a recommended reading list on educating children at home, which is invaluable reading for parents.

The Welsh government provides information on elective home education with a guidance leaflet for parents and carers who are considering educating their child at home: www.gov.wales/elective-home-education.

The Education Authority in Northern Ireland provides *Guidelines for Elective Home Education* for parents at: www.eani.org.uk/services/elective-home-education.

There is further advice and support for home-educating families in England and Wales from Education Otherwise (www.educationotherwise.org). This also offers an excellent factsheet for parents to understand what home-educating is, along with factsheets for teachers, legal professionals, the public, local authorities and others. In addition, it has links to educational resources useful for home-educating.

Learning at home

Scotland's *Curriculum for Excellence* states that 'Although children spend a lot of time in school, they spend much more time at home.' Such a pertinent statement is true throughout a child's 'normal' school life but especially during the current pandemic. Parents, carers and home are an important part of a child's education. Not only do parents and educators require the resources to encourage and support learning but also the skills to guide the learner and to create the learning environment. It is not an easy task and especially so during a pandemic. None of us have encountered the type of home learning we are all experiencing during COVID-19. Many thousands of children and young people are spending many hours each day viewing online lessons from home. It is an unfamiliar situation for many. There are books on home learning available, but it is unlikely any will have included a guide to learning during this situation. There is some advice becoming available online from many different organisations and most have sensible, practical advice and suggestions. The Royal Academy of Dance (www.royalacademyofdance.org/rad-at-home/tips-and-advice-for-home-study) has a particularly clear and practical set of tips that many parents, teachers and students may find useful and adaptable. There is also practical advice to help children (and their parents) study at home from the BBC (www.bbc.co.uk/bitesize/articles/znsmxyc). In addition, Oak National Academy also offers top tips for parents supporting home learning, giving some sensible pointers for success (www.thenational.academy/blog/top-tips-for-parents-supporting-home-learning). Also look at learning in everyday life on Parentkind (www.parentkind.org.uk/Parents/Make-learning-part-of-life) for practical suggestions of incorporating learning into everyday tasks. While tips on home-schooling for a pandemic may become redundant, knowing how to learn at home will continue to be an invaluable skill to develop and understand.

General sources

This book is about resources specifically for individual subjects or topics, however, there are a few resources worth mentioning that cover a whole range of subjects and that are used widely by children and young people. They are excellent one-stop shops for all subjects.

The fantastic **BBC Bitesize** (www.bbc.co.uk/bitesize/learn) covers all subjects studied at Primary, Secondary and Post 16+ level within all four nations. It allows you to select Primary, Secondary or Post 16+ and then within each level select the year group (key stage). For each key stage within each level, every subject is listed, including all subjects specific to the Northern Ireland, Scottish and Welsh curriculums. There are lessons for each subject with videos, quizzes and activities. Not only is this a must for learning but invaluable for revision, offering GCSE students a mechanism for self-testing. In addition to its impressive coverage, its clear layout and its ease-of-use make it accessible to all ages and abilities. It is highly recommended to every student (and parent and educator too!). There is also the BBC Teach facility offering 1000s of free curriculum-mapped videos, arranged by age-group and subject. Not only a great resource for teachers but for all educators.

Equally impressive is **Oak National Academy** (www.thenational.academy), the online classroom made by teachers, for teachers. It has free, high-quality video lessons and resources that are available throughout 2020/21. It has 10,000 lessons and resources available covering a wide range of subjects, from Early Years Foundation Stage to Year 11. Each of the classroom lessons is usually 60 minutes long and delivered by a teacher, using a pre-recorded video along with quizzes, worksheets and activities. Like BBC Bitesize, it is easy to use with access available to everyone.

Twinkl (www.twinkl.co.uk) is a teacher-created site and includes teaching resources, lesson planning and assessment materials. It covers Primary resources, Secondary resources and resources for parents home-schooling. It is extensive in coverage and the resources offered, requiring a simple registration to have access to the free downloads, and includes all subjects within the school curriculum.

Quizlet (www.quizlet.com) is another excellent resource that offers 1000s of tools to help children and young people learn. It has flashcards, games and study sets covering: Languages; Science; Art and Humanities; Maths; Social Sciences; and some miscellaneous hobbies, sports and computer skills. It also has 10,000 ready-made study sets covering 24 GCSE subjects, aligned to exam board specifications. It is popular with schools especially for encouraging children to test their knowledge.

For more general links to resources for home schooling, **The Council for Subject Associations (CfSA)** (www.subjectassociations.org.uk/cfsa-response-to-covid-19) covers every subject, from EYFS to key stage 4.

Parents may also find **Parentkind** useful (www.parentkind.org.uk/For-Parents/Parent-Hub/Supporting-Learning), the website of the Parent Teacher Associations that offers access to online learning resources that support children's learning. Select Free Resources to support learning and choose from Pre-school and Primary; Secondary; Computer Programming; Maths; Science, Technology, Maths and Engineering (STEM); Literacy and English; Staying Active; Art and Creativity; News, audio books and other great stuff!; Northern Ireland and Wales. There is also a link to Handy Resources and links for parents (www.parentkind.org.uk/Parents/Handy-resources-and-links-for-parents). This includes downloadable Parentkind 'how to...' guides.

There are also some standard tools to have to hand. Most of us will have a dictionary lurking at home somewhere, although less so as we turn to online and rely on our technology to correct spelling. However, it is worth mentioning the **Oxford English Dictionary Online**. Most public libraries will have a subscription and use will be via a library card allowing free access. Even if you are not a public library user you can access a host of English resources for children and young people via the Oxford English Dictionary website (https://public.oed.com/teaching-resources). It has worksheets and activities for spelling, punctuation and literacy, all available free.

Encyclopedias have certainly found their place online and many public libraries will have access to one as part of their online services. However, there is some limited access to **Encyclopedia Britannica** online (www.britannica.com). It may not be the full premium facility but it does give access to features, videos and podcasts, plus the ability to browse by category ranging from Geography to World History, Literature to Science and a whole lot more in between. For subjects such as Citizenship it is a great resource to dip into.

There is a place too for fact books. **Guinness World Records** (www.guinnessworldrecords.com) offers the Hall of Fame, Guinness World Records news and features online. There is also a **Kids Guinness World Records** site with learning resources for teachers, educators and parents (http://kids. guinnessworldrecords.com/educators). This has been developed to offer a range of resources featuring record holders and famous adjudicators to bring fun and learning into the classroom or at home. Some of the resources are in partnership with Twinkl Educational Publishing and are especially for primary-age children, with the aim of encouraging and empowering children to develop a growth mindset. They are well worth looking at and with lots of fun and learning guaranteed.

List of organisations included

Aberdeen Archives, Gallery & Museums
ACE Education
Activity Alliance
ADHD Foundation
Aerospace Bristol
Amnesty International UK
Andersen Press
(The) Andrew Carnegie Birthplace Museum
Anti-Bullying Alliance
Anti-Bullying Network
Arbeia Roman Fort
Archaeology Data Service, University of York
Armagh Planetarium
ASH (Action on Smoking and Health)
Ashmolean Museum, Oxford
Association of the British Pharmaceutical Industry
Association for Science Education
Avert
Avoncroft Museum

Baltic Centre for Contemporary Art, Gateshead
BananaLink
(The) Bank of England
(The) Barn Owl Trust
Barrington Stoke
Bats Conservation Trust
BBC
Beamish Museum, County Durham
(The) Beatles Story, Liverpool
Belfast Exposed
Ben Uri - The London Museum of Jewish Art
Bethlem Museum of the Mind, Kent
(The) Bikeability Trust

HOME-SCHOOL LEARNING RESOURCES

Birmingham Museums
Blackburn Museum
Black Country Living Museum
Black Cultural Archives
Bletchley Park
Bloomsbury Children's Publishing
Blue Cross
BookTrust
Boosey & Hawkes
Bosworth Battlefield Heritage Centre
(The) Bowes Museum, County Durham
(The) Box, Plymouth
Braintree Museum
Brighton and Hove Museum
British Council
British Cycling
British Dyslexia Association
British Film Institute
British Geological Society
British Gymnastics
British Heart Foundation
British Library
British Museum
British Nutrition Foundation
British Red Cross
(The) Brontë Society
Brunel Institute, Bristol
Buglife - The Invertebrate Conservation Trust
BullyingUK
Butterfly Conservation

Cadbury World, Birmingham
CADW
Calderdale Museums
Canal and River Trust
Cardiff Castle
(The) Cartoon Museum
Catholic Agency for Overseas Development (CAFOD)
Cats Protection
Centre for Computing History
Centre for Literacy in Primary Education

Centre of Alternative Technology, Machynlleth
Chatsworth House
Chester Zoo
Chesterfield Museum
Childline
Children's University, Manchester
Christian Aid
Colchester and Ipswich Museums
Co-operative Heritage Trust
Council for Subject Associations
(The) Courtauld Institute of Art
Creswell Crags
Culture North Lanarkshire
Cumberland House Natural History Museum
Cycling Scotland

Dartmoor National Park
(The) D-Day Story, Portsmouth
(The) Deep
Derby Museums
Design Museum
(The) Diana Award
(The) Dinosaur Museum, Dorchester
Disability Sport Wales
Discovery Museum, Tyne and Wear
(The) Dorman Museum, Middlesbrough
Dorset County Museum
Down's Syndrome Association
Durham Cathedral
Durham University
Dyslexia Association
Dyspraxia Foundation

(The) Economist Educational Foundation
Eden Camp, North Yorkshire
Ely Museum, Cambridge
England Netball
English Heritage
English National Opera
European Union

Faber Children's Publishing
Fairtrade Foundation
Family Lives
Florence Nightingale Museum
Football Association
Forestry England

(The) Garden Museum
(The) Geological Society
Glasgow Museums
(The) Glasgow Women's Library
Great North Museum
Grosvenor Museum

Hackney Museum
Harper Collins Children's Books
Hartlebury Castle, Worcestershire
Hawk and Owl Trust
Henry Moore Foundation
Historic Environment Scotland
Historic Royal Palaces
Holst Museum
House of Illustration
HSBC UK British Cycling

Imperial War Museum
Invertebrate Conservation Trust

Jane Austen's House, Hampshire
Jersey Zoo
Jewish Museum, London
Jodrell Bank
Jorvik Viking Centre
Jurassic Coast Trust

Kew Gardens
Kidscape
KidsHealth

Lakeside Arts, University of Nottingham
Leeds Museums & Galleries

Life Science Centre, Newcastle upon Tyne
Lion Salt Works, West Cheshire
(The) Literacy Shed
Little Tiger
Liverpool Museums Living Streets
Lloyds Bank Academy
London Canal Museum
London Grid for Learning
London Philharmonic Orchestra
London Transport Museum
London Zoo
Lyme Regis Museum

Macclesfield Museum
Maidstone Museum
(The) Mammal Society
Manchester Museum
Manchester University
Mathematical Association
Mathematics Education Innovation (MEI)
Mentally Healthy Schools
Met Office
Museum of Brands
Museum of Design in Plastic, Arts University, Bournemouth
Museum of East Asian Art, Bath
Museum of Leathercraft
Museum of London
Museum of Zoology, Cambridge
Museum on the Mound, Edinburgh

NASA
National Archives
National Association for Special Educational Needs
National Association for the Teaching of English
National Autistic Society
National Centre for Computer Education
National Civil War Centre
National Coal Mining Museum
National Galleries Scotland
National Geographic Kids
(The) National Football Museum

(The) National Gallery
(The) National Holocaust Centre
National Library of Scotland
National Library of Wales
National Literacy Trust
National Mining Museum Scotland
National Motor Museum
National Museum Cardiff
National Museum of Computing
National Museum Scotland
National Parks
National Poetry Day
(The) National Portrait Gallery
National Roman Legion Museum
National Space Centre
(The) National Theatre
(The) National Trust
National Videogame Museum
National Wool Museum, Wales
Natural History Museum
New Hall Art Collection, Cambridge University
Newcastle University
NHS
(The) Nobel Prize
Norfolk Museum
Northern Ireland War Memorial Museum
Norwich Castle
Nosy Crow
NSPCC

Office for National Statistics
(The) Olympic Museum
Opera North
Oxfam
Oxford University Museum of Natural History
Oxford University Press

Partnership for Children
Pembrokeshire Coast National Park
Pen Museum
People's History Museum

(The) Poetry Archive
(The) Poetry Foundation
(The) Poetry Society
(The) Poetry Zone
Portsmouth Museum
(The) Postal Museum

(The) Quilters' Guild

RAF
(The) Reading Agency
REME (Royal Electrical and Mechanical Engineer Corps)
Richard III Experience
RNLI
Roald Dahl Museum and Story Centre
(The) Roman Baths, Bath
Royal Academy of Dance
Royal Albert Hall
Royal British Legion
Royal College of Music
Royal Geographic Society
Royal Horticultural Society
(The) Royal Institution
Royal Mint
Royal Museums Greenwich
Royal National Institute for the Blind
Royal Opera House
Royal Shakespeare Company
Royal Signals Museum
Royal Society for the Protection of Birds (RSPB)
Royal Society of Chemistry
RSPCA

Salcombe Museum
Salisbury Museum
Save the Children
Scarborough Museums
Scholastic
(The) Science and Engineering Education Research and Innovation Hub (SEERIH)
Science Oxford
Scottish Book Trust

Scottish Poetry Library
(The) Scout Association
Screen Online
Sea City Museum
SENSE (Centre for Satellite Data in Environmental Science)
Seven Stories, the National Centre for Children's Books
Shakespeare Birthplace Trust
(The) Shakespeare Globe Trust
Simon & Schuster
Southampton City Art Gallery
Sport England
Sport Wales
St Fagan's National Museum of History
St John Ambulance
St Paul's Cathedral
STEM Learning
(The) Story Museum, Oxford
Sustain
Sustrans
Swim England
Swindon Art Gallery

Tank Museum
Tate Gallery
Think Campaign, Department of Transport
ThoughtBoxEducation
Time to Change
Titanic Belfast
Transport for London
Trinity House

Usborne Books
UKCIS - UK Council for Internet Safety
UK Coaching
UK Parliament
United Nations
University of Cambridge
University of Cambridge Museums

Victoria and Albert Museum
Victoria Gallery and Museum, Liverpool
Vindolanda Charitable Trust

Water Aid
Weiner Holocaust Library, London
Welsh Government
Welsh National Opera
Welsh Water
Westminster Abbey
Wetland and Wildlife Trust
(The) Wildlife Trusts
William Morris Society
Winchester Science Centre
Winsor & Newton
Woodland Trust
Worcester Art Gallery
Worcester Medical Museum
World Book Day
World Cancer Research Fund
World Wildlife Fund

York Art Gallery
York Museums Trust
Yorkshire Water
Young Citizens
Young Kennel Club
Young Minds
Young People's Trust for the Environment
Youth Sport Trust

A–Z of subjects

ANIMALS, BIRDS, FISH AND PETS

See also: Citizenship - animal rights; Nature

There is no doubt that there's plenty of information about animals, birds, fish and pets to be found from books, magazines and, of course, the internet. To avoid being overwhelmed - and if you are simply wanting factual information on different animals - you could try one of the online encyclopedias, such as **The Online Animal Encyclopedia** (www.aboutanimals.com). You could also use **National Geographic** - either www.nationalgeographic.com/animals/birds for bird pictures and facts or www.nationalgeographic.com/animals/fish for fish. For information looking at a specific animal in more depth or accompanied by a learning activity, try the suggestions below.

Animals

Information

The Deep: A–Z animals

www.thedeep.co.uk/plan-your-visit/meet-our-animals

Learn about the creatures of The Deep and the habitats they live in.

The Mammal Society

www.mammal.org.uk

Click 'Discover Mammals' for a list of all 90 species of mammals in the British Isles. Then click on the mammal picture for information and a downloadable factsheet.

Oxford University Museum of Natural History: learning zone

www.oum.ox.ac.uk/thezone

Designed for younger children to find facts and information on animals.

Young RSPCA

https://young.rspca.org.uk/kids

This has animal information covering pets, wildlife and farm animals.

Learning resources and activities

Animal habitats

www.abpischools.org.uk/topic/animal-habitats/1/1

A great resource from the Association of the British Pharmaceutical Industry looking at human and animal habitats to explore and consider different environments and the animals that live there.

Bats

www.bats.org.uk/resources

This has great resources for families and teachers looking at bats in the context of wildlife conservation. For teachers and educators, select Education and Outreach Resources, then Resources for Teachers/Youth Leaders. For families, select Bats for All Resource Pack and/or Fun Craft activities. However, families, teachers and educators could use all three for inspiring children to look at bats and the environment. Some of the bat crafts would be great for Halloween activities.

Canal & River Trust: learning resources

www.canalrivertrust.org.uk/explorers/resources

This is an excellent learning resource with a wealth of downloadable activities and information. Using the filter, select either Animals or Habitats for activity sheets such as the Water Birds Spotter Sheet. Excellent.

Chester Zoo: learning resources

www.chesterzoo.org/schools/resources

Chester Zoo has over 200 downloadable resources for learning and teaching at home or at school. The extensive range of topics includes: Biodiversity; Climate; Conservation; Endangered Animals and Rainforests, along with many others. Search by age group; curriculum subject; resource type; or topic. Excellent.

Colchester and Ipswich Museums: animal activities

www.cimuseums.org.uk/museumfromhome

This has a host of downloadable activities related to animals including How to Make a Bird Feeder, Pancake Animals and How to Make a Dancing Woolly Mammoth. Great ideas and fun for all the family.

Co-operative Heritage Trust: animals

www.co-operativeheritage.coop/homeschooling-resources

An interesting resource from the Co-operative Heritage Trust for KS1 looking at animal co-operation and co-operative behaviours. Select KS1_Science CHT Co-operative_Animals_Worksheet.pdf.

Get curious! Animal senses

www.museums.norfolk.gov.uk/norwich-castle/learning/learning-at-home

An inspiring set of info-activity sheets to find out about different animals and the senses they rely on. The resources use craft, drama, games and song ideas to develop enquiry and discovery. Suitable for 3-7-year-olds. Excellent.

Ice Age animal factsheets

www.creswell-crags.org.uk/education/teaching-resources

Select Ice Age Animal Factsheets from the list of downloads.

Jersey Zoo: animal fun factsheets

www.durrell.org/wildlife/visit

Learn lots of interesting facts about some unusual animals as well as Rainforests, Habitats and Animal Adaptation. Select Education, then Kids' Zone, then Animals.

London Zoo: online resources

www.zsl.org/zsl-london-zoo/zsl-london-zoo-online-resources

London Zoo has some great online resources for use independent of a visit to the zoo.

Museum of Zoology: Cambridge safari trail

www.museum.zoo.cam.ac.uk/visit-us/museum-trails-and-gallery-map

A downloadable trail developed by the Museum of Zoology highlighting the animals in the architecture in the city centre. Great for families and school trips if you live in Cambridge and an inspired idea to use if you live elsewhere.

Natural History Museum: British wildlife

www.nhm.ac.uk/discover/british-wildlife.html

The Natural History Museum provides a vast array of information and activities on wildlife in the UK.

World Wildlife Fund (WWF)

www.worldwildlife.org/teaching-resources

There is a huge number of educational resources from the WWF. For teachers and parents there is the Wild Classroom, connecting educators with the tools and resources to help children explore and understand the world around them. For those learning at home or looking for activities to do, there are weekly activity plans. In addition, there is the Lesson Library for primary and secondary pupils offering toolkits for the Tiger; Polar Bear; Sea Turtle; Elephant; Dolphin; and Biodiversity. Excellent.

Birds

Information

Hawk and Owl Trust

www.hawkandowltrust.org

From the main menu, select About Birds of Prey for an A–Z of information by bird.

Pocket Guide to Birds

www.museum.wales/cardiff/learning/resources

A small downloadable guide to some common garden birds. Select My Pocket Guide to Birds.

Royal Society for the Protection of Birds (RSPB)

www.rspb.org.uk

Select Birds & Wildlife for a bird A–Z and the facility to Identify a bird, along with a whole host of guides, bird song and advice. Excellent.

Learning resources and activities

Barn owl: learning resources

www.barnowltrust.org.uk

A fantastic set of activity sheets, lesson plans and facts. Select Kids' Stuff. In addition, there are also lesson plans on barn owl conservation for Science, Literacy and Numeracy, including educational resources with study ideas and downloadable worksheets.

Evolution of birds

https://brightonmuseums.org.uk/discover/make-learn/home-schooling

Find out how birds evolved from dinosaurs and how they learned to fly. Scroll down the page and select Natural Sciences.

The story of the dodo

www.portsmouthmuseum.co.uk/get-involved/activities/dodo-word-search-and-story

A short story and accompanying word search about the extinction of the dodo.

Pets

Cats Protection: for kids

https://education.cats.org.uk

Children can learn from the Cats Protection about cats with lots of cat-related fun and crafts to do at home, plus lesson plans, interactive activities and engaging videos

Young Kennel Club

www.ykc.org.uk

Select At Home Games and Printables for dog-related activities. The templates of dog faces to colour are very good.

AROUND THE WORLD

Includes Calendars; Dates and Time Zones

When it comes to knowing what time it is at any given moment in any specific country or finding out about holiday or special dates around the world, you'll find what you are looking for in the suggestions below.

Calendars and dates

www.timeanddate.com

This not only has a world clock, time zone maps and calculators but also printable calendars for any country in any year. Each calendar highlights main holidays and observances with the option to add major Jewish, Muslim and Hindu holidays and observances.

Calendars around the world

www.worldatlas.com/articles/countries-that-use-their-own-calendar.html

Provides a list of countries using their own calendar and a brief history.

Awareness days calendar

www.gogivers.org/free-stuff/awareness-days-calendar

Provides a free calendar of awareness days and religious holidays and observances.

Historical anniversaries calendar

www.history.org.uk/primary/resource/9676/historical-anniversaries-calendar

The Historical Association has produced a historical anniversaries calendar. It is a great way to get children and young people interested in a subject or to raise awareness about a particular issue.

Time, time zones and Greenwich Mean Time

www.greenwichmeantime.com

Find out what Greenwich Mean Time is, plus the time and time zone for every country and area of the world. It includes the fascinating history of the calendar systems in use around the world. Select Articles and then Calendars. Here you will also find articles on clocks, time standards and time as a concept.

C ART

See also: Design and Technology

This is a vast subject area that is undertaken for enjoyment and appreciation as well as taught in schools from primary through to GCSE exam level and beyond. For this reason, there is a wealth of information available from books, magazines, blogs, online databases, national organisations, art collections and, of course, the internet. Art has been with us for a long time so this is to be expected! It is navigating through this offering that requires some guidance in order to cherry pick those sources that provide good information, access to searchable collections and resources that support learning or understanding. It is not just about being shown a picture or object, we want to know more.

Art is divided here into several sections looking at the basics first under Information - use this for art definitions and terminology. The Learning Resources and Activities centre around resources for learning or teaching, such as toolkits or activities to support family-learning or family fun because this too is learning and, better still, inspiring. We are fortunate in that many of the UK's national galleries and art collections have created and developed such tools for everyone to use. Some are specific to art themes and those have been sub-divided here by topic. And whilst we all know that art techniques are plentiful on YouTube and Instagram, the suggestions here include an interesting range from many quality-assured organisations and galleries from around the UK.

There are, of course, hundreds of colouring sheets to be found on the internet. There is a small concession made here to a few that are particularly interesting and could possibly be missed!

Information

Art online

www.tate.org.uk

The Tate Gallery art online resource is fabulous. With 78,000 artworks, 4,000 artists and 22,000 archive items, it is a must for any teacher, parent or child looking for a painting or image. To help the search process there is the Art by Theme facility, which has subjects of artworks such as Animals and Art; Black Identities and Art; Weather and Art; and Family and Art, along with many more.

Art glossary

www.nationalgalleries.org/art-and-artists

Online art glossary from National Galleries Scotland. Explore over 100 terms and discover related artists and artworks. Excellent. The Glossary can be found in the Art & Artists section.

Art terms

www.tate.org.uk/art/art-terms

The Tate's online glossary contains definitions, most with illustrations, of over 400 terms, including artist groups and art movements, techniques, media and other art jargon. Invaluable for those teaching and studying art.

Web Gallery of Art

www.wga.hu

This is a virtual museum and searchable database of European painting and sculpture from the 3rd to 19th centuries. It is an art history resource for students and teachers, as well as young people and parents. Excellent.

Web Museum, Paris

www.ibiblio.org/wm/paint

This provides information on types of paintings by themes and artists. It would be useful as a starting point for school projects. There are some images, but it is mainly text.

Learning resources and activities

Art in the Open

www.benuri.org/schoolsandfamilies

Art in the Open is a teaching resource from Ben Uri - the London Museum of Jewish Art - and the London Grid for Learning. It has three teaching themes: A Sense of Place; Relationships; and Movement. There are lesson plans including activities and discussion topics that support the Programme of Study for Art & Design KS1 and KS2. Excellent.

Ashmolean Museum, Oxford: learning resources

www.ashmolean.org/learning-resource-secondary-art-and-design

Secondary art and design learning resources.

Baltic Art: family activities

www.baltic.art/family-activities

A series of meet and make online activities from artists from Baltic Art. Also, use the Home and School Resources (www.baltic.art/whats-on/home-school) for some interesting art activities, including Tree Textures, Mandala Making and a Resourceful Rainforest.

Courtauld: primary learning resources

www.courtauld.ac.uk/learn/primary-learning-resources

The Courtauld's learning department has designed a series of learning resources using art history and art-based approaches to explore the intentions and processes behind works of art. It includes: Create A View from A Window inspired by Camille Pissarro; Make A Story Picture inspired by Edouard Manet; Create an Albarello Jar inspired by the Maiolica Ceramics; and Create A Geometric Tile inspired by Islamic Patterns. Excellent.

Culture Street: art

www.culturestreet.org.uk

For art students, children and young people who love art, teachers delivering or using art at school and for parents and children learning at home, Culture Street is a must. It is packed with art and artist information using video and lesson plans. There are workshops with videos on how to do screen printing to animation, from digital photography to wire sculpture. There are a host of lesson plans, not only fantastic for teachers but invaluable for learning at home and for parents and children with an interest in the visual arts. Excellent and well worth a visit.

History of art

www.ashmolean.org/learning-resource-history-art

This has downloadable learning resources, including images and videos for art history.

Museum Crush: art

www.museumcrush.org/category/art

Museum Crush offers a wealth of quick reads on art drawn from collections throughout the UK. From Victorians to Pop Art, from metalwork to Slipware Pottery and Ancient Sculpture, Textiles and Photography, along with named artists, photographers, collectors and curators. Without a doubt a superb resource for discovery and inspiration for children, parents and teachers alike.

National Gallery: take one picture

www.nationalgallery.org.uk/learning/take-one-picture

This resource from the National Gallery provides downloads for teachers to use with individual pictures selected for the *Take One Picture* programme. Each year one painting is selected for the programme, with all previous years' picture resources available to download. For each key stage, the resource provides information about the painting and the artist and starting points for discussion. It also suggests lines of enquiry using the picture. An extensive resource for using paintings in the classroom. Select Teachers' Notes.

National Galleries Scotland: art by subjects

www.nationalgalleries.org/art-and-artists

The collection at National Galleries Scotland is available online and is arranged by subject. This is a fantastic resource for art students and a great resource for families and teachers to use for creative writing inspiration.

National Portrait Gallery: art

www.npg.org.uk/learning/digital/art

Select Learning then Digital Resources. The National Portrait Gallery has developed downloadable PDFs, audio and web-based resources to support learning around portraiture and the gallery's collections and exhibitions. As a resource for art, it is fantastic. It has interviews via audio resources with artists and sitters, both contemporary and from the past. There are also resources to investigate various art themes, including Art Techniques; Image & Identity; Portrait Photography; and the Practice of Portraiture. Excellent.

Primary school teaching ideas

www.teachingideas.co.uk

Select Art for a host of downloadable activities, lesson plans and resources. Not only an invaluable resource for teaching but also for parents and children learning from home.

Show Me – part of Culture24

www.show.me.uk/section/art

A wealth of art activities, games and teacher notes to explore collections in relation to the art curriculum topics. The range included is fantastic and offers so much to explore not only for teachers but also young people, children and parents. Excellent and well worth a visit.

Southampton City Art Gallery: Let's Make A . . . learning videos and resources

www.southamptoncityartgallery.com/resources

A collection of downloadable instructions and supporting videos showing how to make a whole series of collection-inspired art. In addition, there are videos exploring art by themes such as Exploring Landscape; Exploring Portraits; and Exploring Sculpture. There is also a collection of Quick Art Idea downloads. Excellent.

Swindon Museum & Art Gallery: Art on Tour educational resources

www.swindonmuseumandartgallery.org.uk

These extensive downloadable resources from Swindon Museum & Art Gallery - Art on Tour - are designed to help teachers, parents and other educators bring learning to life through art. There is a wide range of teacher toolkits and learning resources available to provide practical suggestions for developing children's visual literacy and creative skills, including Art Hacks; Teacher Toolkits; Teaching Resources & Inspiration; Learning Resources for Students; and Lesson Planning. They have been created by teachers and can be used from Early Years to GCSE. The focus is on using artworks as a springboard to learning across the curriculum.

Select Learning and Community, then Art on Tour at Home education resources (or visit www. artontour489147035.wordpress.com/education-resources). Excellent.

Tate kids

www.tate.org.uk/kids

Packed with art activities, games and quizzes, information and exploration of art and artists, along with videos to find out more. Excellent.

Victoria and Albert Museum: art resources for primary schools

www.vam.ac.uk/info/teachers-resources-for-primary-schools

The V&A has a number of art lesson plans for KS1 and KS2. These resources support visits to the permanent collections but can equally be used in the classroom to explore the art, design and culture of a number of different countries. There are lesson plans for Japan, the Islamic Middle East, India and China.

Victoria and Albert Museum: art, craft and design resources for secondary schools

www.vam.ac.uk/info/teachers-resources-for-secondary-schools-and-colleges

The V&A has lesson plans for teachers for KS3, KS4 and KS5, looking at aspects of art, craft and design taken from the collections. It covers 20th Century Design; Islamic Art; Pattern in Architecture; Exploring Skylines; Fashion; Photography; and Jewellery. These resources are linked to a museum visit, however there are elements of the resources that can be extracted or re-purposed for learning at home or in the classroom. Well worth a look and has some useful images.

Art by theme

African art

African Art and Design

www.britishmuseum.org/learn/schools/ages-7-11/africa/classroom-resource-africa-art-and-design

A learning resource for KS2, KS3 and KS4 art and design inspired by African art and adornment. It provides powerpoints with images and considerations when studying artefacts.

Asian art

Museum of East Asian Art: resources

www.meaa.org.uk/learning/family

A great set of resources suitable for primary age children. Covers East Asian topics through art and stories from the museum's collections.

Art techniques

Art masterclass: learning tools for artists

www.winsornewton.com/uk/masterclass

These online video masterclasses for artists from Winsor & Newton are really useful learning tools for art students and teachers.

Art skills for teachers

http://artskills.lgfl.org.uk

This fantastic resource has been developed in association with Ben Uri - the London Jewish Museum of Art, the London Grid for Learning and the National Education Network. It has 40 different teaching activities across six topics: drawing; drawing games; painting; 3D skills; collage; and print. All are available to download as PDFs and are equally suitable for use in the home and classroom. Excellent.

Art tips and techniques

www.winsornewton.com/uk/education

Select Guides for a wealth of art tips and techniques from Winsor & Newton. It is especially useful for KS4 and KS5 art students who are experimenting with techniques for GCSE and A Level.

Axel Scheffler: how to draw a Gruffalo

www.bl.uk/childrens-books/videos/axel-scheffler-how-to-draw-a-gruffalo

A video with transcript to show you how to draw the Gruffalo.

Bowes Museum: art resources for young people

www.thebowesmuseum.org.uk/Learn/Young-People/Resources

A great set of video and downloadable instructions for a range of interesting art techniques including Zine-Making and Making Your Own Paints.

Cartoon Museum: drawing resources

www.cartoonmuseum.org/learning-resources

This includes resources to guide drawing caricatures or a sequential cartoon story along with downloadable instructions for drawing figures.

Derwent art techniques

www.derwentart.com/en-gb/c/inspiration/hints-tips/art-at-home

An extensive online collection of how-to tutorials: easy crafts; draw-a-longs and paint-a-longs; top tips; and step-by-step guides.

How to draw a Bowtruckle

www.wizardingworld.com/features/how-to-draw-a-bowtruckle

For Harry Potter fans, the chance to learn how to draw the magical tree-dwelling creature.

Learn to draw classic Pooh

www.royalmint.com/the-royal-mint-experience/events

To celebrate the 2020 Winnie the Pooh 50p coin, the Royal Mint has a learn to draw Winnie the Pooh video to follow.

Poster design: activities

www.ltmuseum.co.uk/activities

Includes several design activities based around London Transport's iconic images and design. Select either Make Your Own Moquette or Design Your Own Roundels.

Printmaking in the primary school through the work of William Morris

www.williammorrissociety.org/educational-resources

A downloadable learning resource to investigate pattern and develop skills and techniques in printmaking, along with discovering the designer William Morris. They have been created for KS2 but could easily be adapted for KS1 and KS3.

Quentin Blake: How to draw

www.roalddahl.com/things-to-do-indoors/video-drawmatilda

Quentin Blake: How to draw

www.roalddahl.com/roalddahl.com/things-to-do-indoors/video-drawwonka

Roald Dahl: create and learn

www.roalddahl.com/create-and-learn

Select Lesson Plans for Titchy Toddlers for pre-school art activities with *The Enormous Crocodile* and *Colourful Creatures*. Can also be used with Reception and KS1 children.

Artists

Arts heroes factsheets

www.yorkmuseumstrust.org.uk/education/schools-2-2/york-art-gallery-downloads/

A series of factsheets, useful as a starting point, on well-known and lesser-known artists whose works are on display at York Art Gallery. These are colourful and nicely produced and include Lowry, Gwen John, van Dyck, Paul Nash, Felicity Aylieff, Wilhelmina Barns-Graham, Jacob Epstein, William Etty and Lucie Rie.

In the process of doing something

www.theboxplymouth.com/schools/learning-resources?key_stage=key-stage-4

This is a series of filmed interviews with a range of artists giving an insight into the creative process. Suitable for KS4.

National Galleries Scotland: artist A–Z

www.nationalgalleries.org/art-and-artists

Browse the collection through an A-Z of artists.

National Geographic Kids: art resources

www.natgeokids.com/uk/teacher-category/art

This covers artists, craft and painting.

Old Master drawings up close

www.chatsworth.org/art-archives/old-master-drawings-up-close

These online resources are aimed at KS4 and KS5 to explore and look closely at drawings by Raphael, Leonardo da Vinci, Rembrandt, and many others. Some of the resources have been based on A Level History of Art specifications.

Paul Gauguin: learning resources

www.braintreemuseum.co.uk/online-educational-resources

This is a learning resource from Braintree Museum to introduce the artist Paul Gauguin and printmaking to children. Select Courtauld and Gauguin Activities for Primary Schools or Courtauld and Gauguin for Secondary Schools.

Scottish artists: online art activities

www.aberdeencity.gov.uk/AAGM/learn/families

A set of thoughtful art explorations of Scottish artists from the collection at Aberdeen Art Gallery. Select Primary (6-11yrs).

Women artists

www.art.newhall.cam.ac.uk/collection

The New Hall Art Collection at Cambridge University is a permanent collection of modern and contemporary art by women. Explore the collection alphabetically by artist's name and by type of artwork.

Bank of England and money

Artworks

www.bankofengland.co.uk/education/home-learning-hub

Discover the Bank of England's art collection with images of 235 artworks complete with full details.

Canal art

Canal art

www.canalrivertrust.org.uk/explorers/resources

Fascinating facts about the origins of 'Roses and Castles' and other traditional canal art. Encourages children to have a go and includes where to see some brilliant examples.

Colouring

Colouring sheets

www.oxforddoodleclub.com/activity-sheets

Colouring sheets to download and print from the British Museum; Pitt Rivers; Ashmolean Museum; Natural History Museum; and other miscellaneous sheets. Useful and interesting to include with topics for younger children.

Museum of Leathercraft: colouring sheets

www.nationalleathercollection.org/museumfromhome

Beautiful colouring sheets inspired by decorative objects from the collection at the National Leather Collection.

Paddington colouring sheets

www.royalmint.com/our-coins/events/paddington/paddington/paddington-scrapbook

Colour in Paddington visiting some of his favourite London locations.

Worcester Art Gallery: colouring sheets

www.museumsworcestershire.org.uk/collections/activities

A small and sophisticated set of colouring sheets of pictures from the collection at Worcester Art Gallery.

Illustration

Axel Scheffler: top 3 tips for budding illustrators

www.bl.uk/childrens-books/videos/axel-scheffler-top-3-tips-for-budding-illustrators

Video includes transcript.

House of Illustration: family learning resources

www.houseofillustration.org.uk/learn/free-family-learning-resources-illustrating-the-curriculum

This has six activities with step-by-step instructions. It includes Botanical Illustrations; Make Your Own Story Tile Game; Pencil Skills; Atmospheric Buildings with Stick and Ink; Expressing Emotion in Pictures; Painted Collage Creatures. There are further downloadable activities for 2-5-year-olds and 5-12-year-olds:

www.houseofillustration.org.uk/learn/free-family-activities-mini-change-makers

www.houseofillustration.org.uk/learn/free-family-activities-imagining-the-future

Excellent.

Viviane Schwarz: how to develop a character

www.bl.uk/childrens-books/articles/interview-with-viviane-schwarz

Viviane Schwarz shows some unusual techniques for coming up with characters. Includes a transcript of the video.

Impressionism

An Impressionist in Wales

www.museum.wales/cardiff/learning/resources

Select An Impressionist in Wales. Aimed at 7-11-year-olds this is a downloadable iBook, eBook or PDF. It covers the Impressionist painter Sisley's visit to Wales and looks at Victorian Wales. An interesting introduction to Impressionism for children.

Islamic art

Art and maths in the Courtauld Collection

www.courtauld.ac.uk/learn/primary-learning-resources

Select Art & Maths. This learning resource shows the connections between art and maths by exploring the Courtauld's collections of Islamic metalwork and Italian Maiolica ceramics. There is a lesson plan and workbook for upper KS2. A fascinating resource to demonstrate the application of maths that can be adapted for use at home or in the classroom.

Geometry and number in Islamic and British arts and crafts

www.williammorrissociety.org/educational-resources

A downloadable learning resource to explore Islamic Art for KS2 and KS3.

Landscape art

Looking at landscapes

www.museums.norfolk.gov.uk/norwich-castle/learning/trails-and-resources#teacher_resource_pack_ks1

This is a resource pack suitable for KS2 from Norwich Castle Museum and Art Gallery.

London landscapes

www.bankofengland.co.uk/museum/online-collections/artworks/London-landscapes

A collection of landscapes from the 17th century to the 19th century housed at the Bank of England. They show how London's landscape has changed from the reign of Charles I to Queen Victoria.

Myths and legends

Myths and legends coursework guide

www.tate.org.uk/art/student-resource/exam-help/myths-and-legends

A fantastic online resource from the Tate art gallery for art students of all ages, introducing and showing how artists have been inspired and used myths and legends in their works of art, from classical mythology to legends and folk tales. It includes links to find out more about the artists mentioned. Excellent.

Nature

Art in nature

www.chatsworth.org/your-visit/learning/learning-resources/resources-for-ages-7-11
Chatsworth House have produced a great resource to explore natural and organic form and for children to use their senses. It introduces a range of drawing techniques through creative activities, observing differences and similarities in shape, texture, colour and detail. There are references to artists too. The resource is suitable for KS1 and KS2, for home or classroom use. Select Art in Nature.

The elements

www.tate.org.uk/art/student-resource/exam-help/elements
This resource from the Tate art gallery looks at exploring the elements of nature from the weather to the four elements - fire, water, air and earth. It provides links to the artists mentioned and related reading. An excellent resource for GCSE and A Level students of art and design.

Recovery curriculum: arts activities

www.museumsandgalleries.leeds.gov.uk/engage/learn/recovery-curriculum
Arts activities and tutorials themed on the Natural World.

Pop art

Pop art

www.bl.uk/teaching-resources/va-pop-art
This is a teaching resource for 16-18-year-olds from the British Library on pop art. Also linked to the online resources.

Toys

www.tate.org.uk/art/student-resource/exam-help/toys
A student resource on the theme of toys in art from pop art to gender politics. It explores art and the artists with links to find out more. A great resource for GCSE and A Level students.

Portraits and identity

Courtauld: portraiture toolkit

www.courtauld.ac.uk/learn/schools-colleges-universities/learning-resources
Select the Courtauld portraiture toolkit for detailed practical activities using art history skills as well as collage, printing and sketchbook skills. Excellent.

GCSE art and design support materials

www.museums.norfolk.gov.uk/norwich-castle/learning/trails-and-resources#teacher_resource_pack_ks1

Select either Natural Forms or Personal Identity. A lot of the information in these two resources is good advice for GCSE pupils. The resources provide structured activities and guidance. Although the examples are from the Norfolk Museums, the resource itself is adaptable for other artworks.

Looking at portraits

www.museums.norfolk.gov.uk/norwich-castle/learning/trails-and-resources#teacher_resource_pack_ks1

This is an art resource pack from Norwich Castle Museum and Art Gallery suitable for KS2.

Portraits and identity

www.benuri.org/schoolsandfamilies

This substantial learning resource from Ben Uri - the London Jewish Museum of Art - and the London Grid for Learning contains starting points for portraiture and identity projects to do in the classroom or at home. It includes notes about selected works from the Ben Uri collection. It is suitable for KS2-KS4, with information, downloadable lesson plans and twelve classroom activities along with teacher notes. Excellent.

Understanding portraits

www.chatsworth.org/your-visit/learning/learning-resources/resources-for-ages-7-11

For children to look at key characteristics of portraits and to carry out a series of studies to create a mask that represents an identity of themselves or someone they know. A fun way to understand portraits. Select Portraits and Identity. Excellent.

Poster art

Olympic posters

www.olympic.org/museum/visit/schools/teaching-resources/support-de-cours/olympic-posters

Includes a history of the Olympic posters, including poster making techniques, how the design is chosen and the role of the posters. Also includes activities.

Surrealism

Surrealism and design

www.vam.ac.uk/articles/surrealism-and-design

An excellent detailed explanation of Surrealism and the influence on ballet, objects, interiors, graphic design and fashion.

War art

British art of the First World War

www.iwm.org.uk/learning/resources/british-art-of-the-first-world-war

A fantastic learning resource looking at art from World War 1. It provides colour images, artist and picture information and a downloadable PDF of suggested activities. It also includes a film clip of the unveiling of the Cenotaph in Whitehall, London, in 1920. Excellent.

Contemporary art and war

www.iwm.org.uk/learning/resources/contemporary-art-and-war

A learning resource using artwork and interviews with artists looking at contemporary art and war.

The Holocaust through art

http://benuriholocaust.lgfl.org.uk

This programme is designed to help GCSE students deconstruct the relevant works of the Ben Uri collection as a stimulus for their own understanding of the period. As a result, they will gain an insight into pre- and post-war life in Central Europe, artists and their subject matter. There are 15 discussion sheets on 15 artworks, including an overview of the artist and discussion of the composition, materials, content and ideas. There are an additional five activity packs to explore, with all documents and images available to download. The resource is suitable for supporting Holocaust studies for GCSE Art & Design. Excellent.

BOOKS, READING AND STORIES

When it comes to finding out about books or for ideas to inspire reading, we are spoilt for choice. Not only does the UK have some amazing national organisations dedicated to children's reading but we also have our national libraries and public library services, all of them supporting and inspiring reading for children and young people. To find your nearest local library enter your postcode at **www.gov.uk/local-library-services**.

There is also the UK publishing industry, with children's book publishers exemplary in their creation of materials to support their book titles. There are a host of learning toolkits, lesson plans and reading related activities given in the Learning Resources and Activities section below, which is complemented by the resources covered in the Publisher's Learning Resources section. Both of these sources will continue to grow, develop and change as new reading themes and books take centre stage; however, their ability to promote books to children and nurture a love of reading remains constant and of continued importance.

There is further reading guidance in the section on Book Recommendations, offering access to booklists and book collections. There are a few selected resources that use some of Britain's much-loved book characters or for books that now carry the accolade of 'contemporary classic'. No doubt there are many more of these but those listed are some of the best available for those particular titles. And no guide would be complete without mentioning at least some popular authors by name; those included here are by way of example and you may be able to seek out more. To find others, aim to use official sites - these are often available through an author's publisher.

Books and reading

Learning resources and activities

BookTrust

www.booktrust.org.uk

BookTrust is the UK's largest children's reading charity. This includes top tips for reading, booklists and reading resources. Excellent.

See also:

BookTrust Cymru

www.booktrust.org.uk/what-we-do/booktrust-cymru

BookTrust Northern Ireland

www.booktrust.org.uk/what-we-do/booktrust-ni

Discovering children's books

www.bl.uk/childrens-books

This has resources to explore centuries of stories, poems and illustrations. It has themes to explore and a host of activities for children and young people. The theme of Home and Belonging is excellent. It includes interviews with writers and artists and tips on being an author.

Lesson plans using books

www.teachingideas.co.uk/activity-types/book

A host of book ideas complete with lesson plans to use for a range of subjects and topics for KS1 and KS2. This is an excellent resource and packed with ideas for using books. A fantastic website for parents, teachers and librarians. Highly recommended.

National Literacy Trust

www.literacytrust.org.uk/resources

This has a wealth of resources for teachers, educators and parents covering early years, primary and secondary. The National Literacy Trust works to improve reading, writing, speaking and listening in children, young people and adults. Use the Refine facility to search for relevant resources, which include booklists, toolkits and materials. Excellent.

Reading Agency

www.readingagency.org.uk

The Reading Agency has a huge selection of resources to inspire teachers, parents and educators in their use of books with children and young people. Select Resources and then filter by Categories or by Age. It includes activity sheets, booklists and toolkits. Children and young people can use the Find a Book facility to find book recommendations. Excellent.

Scottish Book Trust: learning resources

www.scottishbooktrust.com/learning-resources

This has an extensive range of resources for teachers, educators and parents to inspire reading, develop creative writing and to explore books. The resources range from simple activities to toolkits, lesson plans and shared practice. They are divided by age range for 0-2; 3-5; 6-8; 9-11; 12-14; and 15-18. Excellent.

World Book Day

www.worldbookday.com

Packed with resources, videos, book recommendations and more, this is a fantastic resource for teachers, educators and parents. It can be used all year round and not just for the annual World Book Day - which is the first Thursday in March. Select

Schools for an extensive offering of downloadable resources for early years, primary and secondary. They include activities, posters, ideas and tips for enjoying reading. Parents/carers can also select Families for activities, many of which overlap with the school resources but can be filtered by type of resource (lesson plans, activity sheets and discussion guides). Excellent.

Publishers' learning resources

Andersen Press: resources

www.andersenpress.co.uk/free-stuff

This includes book samplers, discussion guides and activities for a wide selection of Andersen Press children's books.

Bloomsbury Children's Books: activities

www.bloomsbury.com/uk/superpage/activity-packs

Bloomsbury have extensive resources available to support reading and use of their books. They include downloadable colouring sheets, activity packs and posters arranged by age. Excellent.

Bloomsbury Children's Books: resources for teachers, librarians, parents and carers

www.bloomsbury.com/uk/childrens/teachers-librarians-parents-carers

This resource is packed with teaching guides, notes and resources for a long list of Bloomsbury's children's titles. Highly recommended and well worth exploring. Excellent.

Faber children's teaching resources

www.faber.co.uk/faber-childrens-resources

This provides free downloadable resources, including activity and cross-curricular lesson plans on a number of children's books published by Faber. The lesson plans are extensive and great for teachers, parents and librarians. Excellent.

HarperCollins Children's Books: teaching resources

www.harpercollinschildrensbooks.co.uk/free-teaching-resources-activities

This is a fantastic set of free resources and activities to support reading of a large selection of HarperCollins' children's book titles. Excellent.

Have a look also at: **www.harpercollinschildrensbooks.co.uk/fun-and-learning** which has book recommendations and activity sheets for all ages.

Little Tiger: activities and resources

www.littletiger.co.uk/resource-category/activities

A selection of simple activities for children related to books published by Little Tiger.

Nosy Crow: teachers' resources

www.nosycrow.com/teachers-resources

This has classroom resources for a selection of Nosy Crow Books. Excellent. See also: Nosy Crow: activity sheets - **www.nosycrow.com/activity-sheets**.

Oxford University Press: colouring and activity sheets

https://global.oup.com/education/children/free-resources/colouring-sheets

An extensive A–Z of downloadable activity and colouring sheets related to OUP book titles. Fantastic to encourage and support reading.

There are also quizzes at:

https://global.oup.com/education/children/free-resources/quizzes

And related craft activities at:

https://global.oup.com/education/children/free-resources/craft-activities

Oxford University Press: reading notes

https://global.oup.com/education/children/free-resources/reading-notes

A great resource of downloadable reading notes arranged A–Z on an extensive list of book titles, including *The Kite Rider*, *Tom's Midnight Garden*, *White Dolphin* and many more. Excellent.

Penguin: children's articles and activities

www.penguin.co.uk/articles/children.html

This has activities, quizzes, book recommendations, videos and podcasts for children and families.

Simon & Schuster: activity sheets

www.simonandschuster.co.uk/c/Activity-Sheets

An excellent set of activity sheets based on books published by Simon & Schuster. Some have teacher notes that can be used by educators and parents.

Usborne Books: teachers' resources

www.usborne.com/gb/activities-for-kids

This has a fantastic set of resources for teachers and educators that includes lesson plans and activities to support a selection of Usborne books. Excellent.

Book recommendations (booklists and book collections)

1001 stories collection

www.storymuseum.org.uk/1001-stories

If you need ideas for books to read or recommend, the searchable collection from the Story Museum is a must. Search by story form, e.g. novels, picture books or poems, among a host of others, or by theme, e.g. action and adventure, magic or historical.

Black Lives Matter: booklists for ages 0–16+

www.literacytrust.org.uk/resources/black-lives-matter-book-lists-ages-0-16

All the books listed are by black authors and/or illustrators. They are divided by age 0-4; 5-8; 9-12; 13-16 and 16+ and can be used to support home or classroom work to explore race and identity.

Black stories matter

www.sevenstories.org.uk/learning/books-and-resources/black-stories-matter

This provides a list of books for children of all ages by black authors and illustrators and about black people in history. Excellent.

BookTrust: great book guide

www.booktrust.org.uk/books-and-reading/our-recommendations/great-books-guide

As well as the annual book guide, BookTrust has a wealth of themed booklists. By using the filter facility, it is possible to select booklists by age or by keyword.

Centre for Literacy in Primary Education (CLPE): booklists

www.clpe.org.uk/library/booklists

CLPE has a wealth of booklists covering a wide range of topics, themes and authors, including Black History, Refugee Experience, Norse Myths, The Environment, Arthurian Legends, Michael Foreman and Lauren Child, along with many more. Excellent.

COVID-19 booklist to support children and families

www.reading-well.org.uk/news/covid19children

This booklist has been created in partnership with ASCEL (Association of Senior Children's and Education Librarians), Libraries Connected and the Reading Agency. Many of the books included are available from the publishers as free downloadable e-books and have been created specially to support children and young people during COVID-19. Excellent.

Diverse Voices: resource packs

www.sevenstories.org.uk/learning/books-and-resources/diverse-voices-free-resources

Downloadable resource packs exploring the theme of 'Home'. Covers Early Years, KS1, KS2 and KS3.

Good books for tough times

www.partnershipforchildren.org.uk/what-we-do/resources-for-parents/good-books-for-tough-times.html

Recommendations for ages 5-8 and 9-12. Both lists provide book titles to use with children as a starting point for talking about issues they may be worried about or living with. It would benefit from updating but does include lots of excellent books.

Holocaust Memorial Day

www.literacytrust.org.uk/resources/holocaust-memorial-day

A learning resource for schools and families to encourage discussion on the Holocaust.

Love my books

www.lovemybooks.co.uk

Fantastic for books and includes activities and discussion points. Suitable for 0–11 years. It has a host of top ten lists of reads, along with books by theme such as dinosaurs, heroes and villains, space, special times and more.

Malorie Blackman: learning activities

www.scottishbooktrust.com/learning-resources/malorie-blackman-learning-activities

An excellent resource from the Scottish Book Trust to explore Malorie Blackman's book *Noughts and Crosses*. It can be used to consider the themes of equality, conflict and political activism.

Reading – war

www.barringtonstoke.co.uk/reading-war

This is an online resource using two titles from publisher Barrington Stoke. It includes information on the themes explored in *Over the Line* by Tom Palmer and *Tilly's Promise* by Linda Newbery. Both are suitable for reluctant or dyslexic readers.

Reading Well for children

www.reading-well.org.uk/children

Reading Well for children is a quality-assured book collection for children 7–11 years old to support mental health and wellbeing. All the books included have been chosen and recommended in partnership with the Reading Agency by professional health organisations, including the NHS, Public Health England and Young Minds, and co-produced with children and young people.

Reading Well for young people's mental health

www.reading-well.org.uk/books/books-on-prescription/young-people-mental-health

This selection from Reading Well is for young people from 13–18 years. The books included in the collection provide advice and information about issues such as anxiety, stress, OCD, eating disorders, bullying, along with other difficult experiences. All the books included have been chosen and recommended in partnership with the Reading Agency by professional health organisations, including the NHS, Public Health England and Young Minds, and co-produced with young people.

Story explorer

www.amnesty.org.uk/resources/story-explorer-questions-exploring-fiction

Story explorer is a downloadable resource to explore human rights themes in fiction, with questions designed to promote discussion and critical thinking.

Twinkl book list

www.twinkl.co.uk/book-list

A great range of themed booklists. Select either EYFS, KS1 or KS2 and then the chosen theme or topic for a list of titles.

Books by author

Children's Laureate

www.booktrust.org.uk/what-we-do/childrens-laureate

Find out about the current Children's Laureate Cressida Cowell, as well as discovering all previous Children's Laureates from the past 20 years. A great way to find out more about some brilliant children's authors and illustrators such as Michael Rosen, Lauren Child and Chris Riddell, plus the seven other recipients of this prestigious title. The role of the Children's Laureate is awarded once every two years to a writer or illustrator of children's books to celebrate outstanding achievement in their field. Excellent.

Enid Blyton

www.enidblyton.co.uk

Enid Blyton remains a firm favourite with children. For fans young and old, this offers lots of information and activities, as well as learning resources with lesson plans for using at school, at home or within a library.

Jacqueline Wilson

www.penguin.co.uk/puffin/jacqueline-wilson.html

For Jacqueline Wilson fans this is a must. Packed with things to do and read. Excellent.

Julia Donaldson: learning activities

www.scottishbooktrust.com/learning-resources/julia-donaldson-activity-packs

These are activities to use with four of Julia Donaldson's books. Suitable for children 3-8 years old.

Michael Morpurgo

www.michaelmorpurgo.com

Select Resources for a wealth of teaching resources on over 40 of Michael Morpurgo's books. Search by KS2 or KS3 or by one of two topics - Times of War or Animals. Excellent.

Roald Dahl: A–Z of stories and books

www.roalddahl.com/roald-dahl/stories

An A-Z timeline of Roald Dahl stories and books. Excellent.

Children's classic and contemporary classic books

Charlie and the Chocolate Factory: family activities

https://museums.calderdale.gov.uk/toffee-town-activities

This is a set of chocolate-related activities based on the Mackintosh Toffee and Quality Street chocolates manufactured in Halifax. They have been linked to the Roald Dahl children's book *Charlie and the Chocolate Factory*.

Harry Potter

www.wizardingworld.com

A must for Harry Potter fans, packed with quizzes, crafts, information and chapter videos.

The Jolly Postman – learning resource

www.postalmuseum.org/visit-us/schools/learning-resources

Select *The Jolly Postman* for a lovely learning resource from the Postal Museum designed for EYFS and KS1 Literacy. It includes teachers' notes, interactive powerpoints and activity ideas using the fictional narrative of *The Jolly Postman* and the real history of the post.

Kenneth Grahame's Wind in the Willows character masks

www.bankofengland.co.uk/education/home-learning-hub

Select Family Fun, then go to Character Masks.

Paddington's adventures at The Tower of London

www.royalmint.com/the-royal-mint-experience/events

Bring Paddington to life and have some great fun at home with this play resource from the Royal Mint. Great for younger children.

Peter Rabbit

www.nationaltrust.org.uk/features/peter-rabbit-activities-and-games-to-try-at-home

This has Peter Rabbit activities and games to do at home, plus five downloadable activity packs for Beatrix Potter characters - Peter Rabbit and Mrs Tiggy-Winkle; Squirrel Nutkin and Mr McGregor; Flopsy, Mopsy and Cotton-Tail and Jemima Puddle-Duck; Benjamin Bunny and Snow Rabbit; Mrs Tittlemouse and Mr Jeremy Fisher.

Private Peaceful: activity sheets

www.harpercollinschildrensbooks.co.uk/free-teaching-resources-activities

Download this wonderful resource for 7-12-year-olds to support the use of Michael Morpurgo's classic *Private Peaceful* in conjunction with the World War 1 history topic.

Roald Dahl: create and learn

www.roalddahl.com/create-and-learn
This has lesson plans for three of Roald Dahl's classics: *Charlie and the Chocolate Factory; Matilda;* and *The Witches.* Excellent.

The Tiger Who Came to Tea: activities

www.tigerwhocametotea.com/activities
Colouring sheets, word search and other activities for young children (and adults too!).

BULLYING

See also: PSHE (Personal, Social, Health and Economic Education)

The issue of bullying is covered in the curriculum subject of PSHE, however as this is not just a school issue, the resources that offer information, advice and learning materials are listed below. There are a number of national organisations who are working with parents, teachers and educators to both support and empower children and young people to understand and reject bullying.

Information

Anti-Bullying Alliance

www.anti-bullyingalliance.org.uk/tools-information

This is packed with information for parents, teachers and young people on every aspect of bullying, all of which is clearly presented and well organised. Excellent.

Anti-Bullying Network

www.antibullying.net

The Anti-Bullying Network was set up by the University of Edinburgh in 1979. It has information on all forms of bullying with information for young people, educators, teachers and parents/carers. It includes printable information sheets and signposting to other organisations and websites. However, although the site is still available and the information sheets give good advice, the site does not appear to have been added to since 2017 and this should be kept in mind.

Bullying UK

www.bullying.co.uk

This provides advice for young people, parents and schools.

NSPCC: bullying and cyberbullying

www.nspcc.org.uk/what-is-child-abuse/types-of-abuse/bullying-and-cyberbullying

This provides information and advice for parents and carers on all aspects of bullying. Excellent.

See also:

NSPCC: Stop Speak Support school pack

https://learning.nspcc.org.uk/research-resources/schools/stop-speak-support-school-pack

Stop, Speak, Support was developed by the NSPCC and the Royal Foundation Taskforce on the Prevention of Cyberbullying. It is aimed at 11 - 16-year-olds, who are 'bystanders' of online bullying. This downloadable school pack contains activities and resources for teachers to use with key stage 3 and 4.

Bullying, abuse, safety and the law

www.childline.org.uk/info-advice/bullying-abuse-safety

This is packed with information on all types of bullying, abuse, online and mobile safety and crime and the law.

Learning resources and activities

Anti-Bullying from The Diana Award

www.antibullyingpro.com

The Diana Award Anti-Bullying campaign engages young people, parents and teachers to change the attitudes, behaviour and culture of bullying by building skills and confidence to address different situations both online and offline. The resources are fantastic, beautifully produced and simply require a request for the download. There is a prolific number of resources on offer, covering all forms of bullying, and a range of formats, including videos, guides, activities, presentations and lesson plans. Fantastic for either classroom or home use.

Bullying and Down's Syndrome

www.downs-syndrome.org.uk/for-families-and-carers/emotional-well-being-resources

This is a teaching resource for understanding different types of bullying and what a person with Down's Syndrome should do if they are being bullied. Select Bullying from the accessible Emotional and Wellbeing resources and then download for free from the online shop.

Bullying UK

www.bullying.co.uk

This provides advice and resources for young people, parents and educators. It also has anti-bullying resources to download. Excellent.

Kidscape: resources for help with bullying

www.kidscape.org.uk

This is packed with resources and advice for young people, parents and educators.

Partnership for Children

www.partnershipforchildren.org.uk/what-we-do/anti-bullying-week-2020.html

This provides a downloadable resource for primary children to look at bullying.

Talk about bullying

https://oxfamilibrary.openrepository.com/handle/10546/620880

This provides a series of lessons from Oxfam Education, suitable for use with 6-8-year-olds and enables children to explore their experiences of bullying using a series of themes which includes fairness, hurtful statements, and feelings and resolutions.

CHANGE AND LOSS (INCLUDING BEREAVEMENT)

See also: PSHE (Personal, Social, Health and Economic Education)

Change and loss in a child's or young person's life either through death, divorce, separation or family strife is never an easy issue to discuss. Some aspects can be covered through the PSHE curriculum and it is worth looking at resources within the main toolkits there. Useful too are the book suggestions within the Reading Well Collection for Children (**www.reading-well.org.uk/children**) dealing with bereavement.

Learning resources and activities

Change and loss

www.partnershipforchildren.org.uk

Select What We Do/Resources for Parents, then select Resilience-building Activities for a set of downloadable resources dealing with feelings; communication; friendship; dealing with anger; and change and loss. Select Change and Loss for resources on grieving to use with children from 5–9 years.

Child Bereavement UK

www.childbereavementuk.org

Packed with information and resources to deal with coping with grief and loss, including COVID-19 resources for young people. The Path of Grief resource is worth a particular mention. Select the Support & Information menu.

Coping with the death of a loved one

www.partnershipforchildren.org.uk/what-we-do/childrens-wellbeing-activities-for-teaching-staff-and-families.html

These are resources to help children find healthy ways to deal with their feelings and reactions to the COVID-19 pandemic. There are excellent downloadable resources for both teachers and families to use covering issues such as coping with the death of a loved one. Some of the activities are available in other languages, including Bulgarian, Danish, Polish, Portuguese, French and Spanish.

Hope Again

www.hopeagain.org.uk

For young people coping with living after loss.

Recovery curriculum: loss and life for our children and schools post pandemic

www.evidenceforlearning.net/recoverycurriculum#mentalhealth

Looks at the considerations for a recovery curriculum when children and young people return to school post-COVID-19. In addition, provides links to other resources and a list of book recommendations.

Recovering from change and challenges

www.redcross.org.uk/get-involved/teaching-resources/recovering-from-change-and-challenges

This has session plans to explore risk and changes in our lives.

Royal British Legion: Remembrance

www.britishlegion.org.uk/get-involved/remembrance/teaching-remembrance

These resources from the Royal British Legion have been created in partnership with the National Literacy Trust. They include lesson plans that are suitable for school or home learning. There are fantastic materials to download, including Then and Now Assemblies that have been designed for either whole school assemblies, class presentations or to use for learning at home. In addition, there are resources for each key stage, all of which are extensive and simply excellent. All resources are in English and Welsh.

There are also Remembrance resources for Girlguiding, Cadets and Scouts: **www.britishlegion.org.uk/get-involved/remembrance/teaching-remembrance/youth-groups**

Young Minds: grief and loss

www.youngminds.org.uk/find-help/feelings-and-symptoms/grief-and-loss

This website provides an explanation of what grief is and how grieving can feel. It offers an excellent list of organisations with contact details where young people can get help.

C CITIZENSHIP

See also: Bullying; Geography - Weather - Climate Change; Health - Staying safe; History - Black history; History - Women's history - Suffrage

Citizenship has been a school curriculum subject since 2002. For early years and primary, citizenship, which is non-statutory at this age, aims to develop children's social skills and understanding of others whilst sowing the seed to encourage participation in society. For secondary, the statutory programme of study sets out to provide young people with the knowledge, skills and understanding of what it is to be an active citizen. It aims for young people to be aware of and understand democracy, government, justice and the law, human rights and social issues, along with having the ability to develop into competent citizens. Such citizens are able to organise their own finances, analyse information to solve problems and make good choices allowing them to contribute to society. However, in reality, teaching a child citizenship has been around a lot longer than 2002 and most parents or carers would want their child to develop into responsible citizens. It is hoped therefore that these resources are both useful for teachers and educators following curriculum specifications and those parents or young people keen to understand how our society works and the importance placed on each individual to play their part. Further information can be found from the Association of Citizenship Teaching (ACT) (**www.teachingcitizenship.org.uk**).

Fortunately, citizenship learning and teaching has been embraced by many important organisations and institutions, including the British Library, the Economist and Oxfam, and these can be found in the Learning Resources section below. The areas or issues that children and young people are encouraged to have an understanding of are divided into: Animal Welfare; Democracy, Voting and Justice; Farming, Food and Water (to consider food and water poverty, ethical consumerism and food production); Human Rights and Civil Rights; Digital Rights; Equality and Inequality; and Immigration and Refugees. These resources are vast and varied and provide a rich source of facts, discussion and debate.

Information

Christian Aid: primary and secondary school resources

www.christianaid.org.uk/get-involved/schools/primary-teaching-resources
www.christianaid.org.uk/get-involved/schools/secondary-teaching-resources
Excellent teaching resources for pupils to explore and consider world issues and their own role as a global citizen.

Save The Children

www.savethechildren.org.uk/en/online-library.htm

Packed with publications and resources on issues relating to children worldwide. Subjects include child protection; child rights; health and nutrition; education; and child poverty. Some of the publications may be useful for working with KS5.

Learning resources and activities

British Library teaching resources for citizenship

www.bl.uk/teaching-resources?teachingsubjects=citizenship

A huge amount of teaching resources for citizenship covering ages 11-14, 14-16 and 16-18. They are linked to the curriculum and covering topics such as equality and work; freedom; race; and relationships. There are also links to British Library online resources.

The Economist Educational Foundation: learning resources

www.economistfoundation.org/resources/#resources

If anything is going to inform, educate and provide material for discussion for young people about the world they are growing up in, then this is it. The Economist offers a brilliant learning resource that they describe as 'Resources designed for form/pastoral time or for home-learning'. There are resources on racism; COVID-19; freedom of speech; and rights and the internet, amongst others. Not only great for young people but for all parents and educators too. Excellent.

Go-Givers

www.youngcitizens.org/go-givers

Go-Givers is the young citizens KS1 and KS2 programme for teaching citizenship and PSHE. For the 2020/2021 academic year, the Pears Foundation is funding all UK primary schools to have free access to the Go-Givers resources, which are all mapped to the PSHE, RSE and Citizenship programme of study. The list of topics covered is excellent with lesson plans for: my community; what is an infectious disease; children's rights; cultural diversity in the UK; democracy; fake news; migration; and human rights, to name but a few. It also has a series of Ethos Statements that can be printed for classroom displays linked to developing citizenship skills.

In addition, for home learning you can sign up to receive resources taken from KS1 and KS2 that have been adapted to be delivered by parents at home. It also has a great section called Planning, which maps lesson plans from Go-Givers to the new statutory guidance for 2020 for RSE and Health Education and to the updated PSHE study programme for 2020 and to the Citizenship programme. Excellent.

Oxfam Education: global citizenship

www.oxfam.org.uk/education

Packed with resources, lesson plans and activities to use within the classroom or at home, this covers a wealth of topical and contemporary issues to consider as a young citizen of the world. It includes detailed lesson plans and activities on climate change; rights; conflict and disasters; education; governance and citizenship; health; humanitarian; inequality; natural resources; trade; water; sanitation and hygiene; and gender. It does require selecting from a list of documents and reports, otherwise a great resource.

Exploring values through portraiture

www.npg.org.uk/learning/digital/citizenship

A teaching resource looking at shared values to promote a diverse and cohesive society and to shape the future. This provides information, discussion and activities for pupils. It is also a valuable resource for parents, teachers and young people exploring British society and the importance for young people to discuss, question and discover more about their changing world. This can be used in conjunction with a resource called Citizenship and the Arts. Excellent.

People's History Museum: citizenship

www.phm.org.uk

The People's History Museum is dedicated to sharing stories of the revolutionary reformers, workers, voters and citizens who championed for change and rallied for rights and equality. There are lots of online resources designed and developed by the Museum using its extensive collections to explore four centuries of ideas worth fighting for. Excellent and well worth looking at.

Primary school teaching ideas

www.teachingideas.co.uk

Select Citizenship to view resources from the Dogs Trust on citizenship.

Screen online

www.screenonline.org.uk

Select Education for access to films and television titles from 1890 to 2014. Access the Lesson Bank for links to curriculum subjects covering English, History, Geography, Citizenship, Science, Music, Art & Design, MFL and RE, not to mention Film and Media Studies and the Performing Arts. This has some amazing films and documentaries with detailed lesson plans. Fantastic to use in the classroom or for learning at home. Excellent.

Animal welfare

Blue Cross: resources

www.bluecross.org.uk/downloads-teachers-and-groups

The Blue Cross produces teaching resources for all key stages written with teachers. It includes lesson plans from Early Years to KS3 for children to consider responsible ownership. There are also fun downloadable activities.

Cats Protection: resources

https://education.cats.org.uk/teachers

This has downloadable lesson plans using animations, videos, digital activities, quizzes and powerpoints, all linked to the curriculum.

RSPCA

https://education.rspca.org.uk/education/home

This has a wealth of resources for learning about animals and their welfare. There are lesson plans for early years, primary and secondary. In addition, there are resources for the Compassionate Class programme, which encourages children to develop compassion and empathy through animal welfare and is PSHE accredited. There are also interactive resources, all of which can be used in the classroom or for home learning. Excellent.

Democracy, justice and voting

Co-operative Heritage Trust: KS2 Citizenship

www.co-operativeheritage.coop/homeschooling-resources

Select the KS2 Citizenship CHT worksheet.pdf. With this worksheet, children can explore how being co-operative and a good citizen are linked. They can also learn about democracy and how you can use it with co-operation to make positive changes in your life.

Democracy past

www.phm.org.uk/vital-voters/past

Explore 200 years of democracy in Britain and discover with the Vital Voters Vloggers and the People's History Museum why we need the right to have our say. The group researched some key events in Britain's history and discovered how democracy has developed, what it has achieved and why it is important.

Democracy present

www.phm.org.uk/vital-voters/present

Find out how voting works and what Parliament does from the People's History Museum and the UK Parliament. Excellent.

I Want My Hat Back by Jon Klassen

www.amnesty.org.uk/resources/book-and-activities-i-want-my-hat-back

A downloadable resource to support working with younger children using the book *I Want My Hat Back* by Jon Klassen. It explores the concepts of lying, stealing and justice.

Parliament and legislation

https://learning.parliament.uk/en/resources

This provides an extensive collection of resources from the UK Parliament. It covers: what is Parliament; how laws are made; democracy and you; voting; and general elections, along with resources looking at race relations; LGBTQ+; inequality; and Disability. The downloadable resources range from videos, worksheets, presentations, books and information. Many of the resources are also available in Welsh.

Digital rights

My digital rights

www.bl.uk/my-digital-rights

Awarded the ACT Quality Mark for Citizenship Teaching Resources, this learning resource from the British Library looks at young people's rights, responsibilities and online safety.

Diversity, equality and inequality

Disability History Month illustrated book

https://learning.parliament.uk/en/resources/disability-illustrated-book

This has stories of influential people who have had an impact on disability-related UK laws and equal rights. Suitable for KS1 and KS2. Available in Welsh.

Equality and justice curriculum

www.thoughtboxeducation.com/equality-justice-curriculum

This extensive resource from ThoughtBox offers downloadable lessons and resources on equality and justice by age group (5-7, 7-9, 9-11, 11-13, 13-15 and 15-18). It examines the meaning of equality, justice and fairness and uses activities that encourage thinking and empathy. ThoughtBox requires individuals to register to access the free resources, which is well worth doing and is ideal for parents. Excellent.

Film: a language without borders

www2.bfi.org.uk/education-research/education/film-language-without-borders

Using film to explore the experience of children arriving in an unfamiliar place or otherwise having an experience of being different. This has downloadable teaching resources. Excellent.

Influential Black Britons illustrated book

https://learning.parliament.uk/en/resources/influential-black-britons-illustrated-book

This has stories of influential Black Britons who have impacted UK laws and equal rights. It has a downloadable book *Influential Black Britons* and a presentation. It is also available in Welsh. Suitable for KS2 and KS3. Excellent.

Kick

www.amnesty.org.uk/resources/book-and-activities-kick
A downloadable resource to support work using the book *Kick* by Mitch Johnson, which explores the imbalance of a world where it takes a Western football star 100 seconds to earn the monthly wage of the child labourers who make football boots.

LGBT+: resources

www.liverpoolmuseums.org.uk/lgbt-resources
Find out about LGBT+ history through resources linked to the stories of Liverpool's lesbian, gay, bi-sexual and trans communities.

Malorie Blackman: learning activities

www.scottishbooktrust.com/learning-resources/malorie-blackman-learning-activities
An excellent resource from the Scottish Book Trust to explore Malorie Blackman's book *Noughts and Crosses*. It can be used to consider the themes of equality, conflict and political activism.

My Hair by Hannah Lee

www.faber.co.uk/faber-childrens-resources
Scroll down Books and select download activity for *My Hair* by Hannah Lee and Allen Fatimaharan.

Votes for women: learning resources

www.phm.org.uk/learn/ideas-worth-exploring/resources-votes-for-women
These are KS3 resources from the People's History Museum to support learning on Women's Suffrage 1900–1918 and the impact on women's rights and equality. In addition, find out more about the campaign for women to have the right to vote in Britain. Excellent.

Farming, food and water

Banana Link

www.bananalink.org.uk
Information about fair trade within the banana industry.

Buoys, beacons and bananas

www.trinityhouse.co.uk/education
Trinity House is responsible for the safety of shipping and seafarers as well as the General Lighthouse Authority (GLA for England & Wales). The educational resources aim to help pupils learn about shipping and seafaring, the importance of the sea to the food we have in our shops and our trade links with the rest of the world. It has downloadable resources for KS1, KS2 and KS3.

Children's Food Campaign

www.sustainweb.org/childrensfoodcampaign

Excellent for exploring children's rights in relation to the food industry and the environment. It looks at food poverty, obesity and food marketing, to name a few. It has publications to download that are worth the time scrolling through. Very useful for teachers to create materials and for KS4 research.

Ethical consumer

www.co-operative.coop/twenty-years-of-ethical-consumerism

A report from the Co-op Food group looking at ethical expenditure and the UK consumer over the past two decades. An interesting report for inclusion with discussion on food and farming topics.

Fair trade

https://schools.fairtrade.org.uk

A wonderful resource from the Fairtrade Foundation where you'll find everything you need to teach and learn about fair trade. The resources, lesson plans and activities cover the issues facing the global society - where our food comes from, interconnectedness, sustainable development and the role of the individual. There are resources for early years, primary and secondary children. There are also films on 'What is Fairtrade?', bananas, cocoa and cotton. In addition, there is a wonderful resource map that allows the user to find teaching and learning resources related to specific regions of the world. Excellent.

Food Waste Warrior Toolkit

www.worldwildlife.org/teaching-resources/toolkits/food-waste-warrior-toolkit

The Food Waste Warrior Toolkit provides lessons, activities and resources for children to look at the impact on our planet from food waste.

Sustainable development

www.nobelprize.org/nobel-prize-lessons-sustainable-development

A lesson plan for teachers from the Nobel Prize on sustainable development. Covers four themes - Saving Lives; Feeding Humanity; Protecting the Planet; and Connecting the World.

Water Aid

www.wateraid.org/uk/get-involved/all/schools-and-teachers

This is packed with resources for schools and home learning. Select either KS1, KS2, KS3 or KS4.

Human rights (includes race and racism)

Anne Frank Trust: changing attitudes

www.annefrank.org.uk

A fantastic resource with downloadable workbooks and activities for children and young people from 9 to 16 years. This learning resource supports families, educators and young people to challenge prejudice and discrimination in today's society. Excellent.

Black British humanitarians

www.redcross.org.uk/get-involved/teaching-resources/celebrating-black-history-month

A fantastic resource from the British Red Cross for secondary pupils to discover some exceptional Black British humanitarians. It enables young people to reflect on the experience of racism and highlights how to talk with children and young people about race and racism.

The Black Curriculum

www.theblackcurriculum.com

This is a social enterprise that aims to deliver black British history across the UK. It has a curriculum and some free resources to use to teach pupils about Black history.

Black Lives Matter: learning resources

www.liverpoolmuseums.org.uk/black-lives-matter

A fantastic collection of resources including books, podcasts and charities brought together by National Museums Liverpool with the aim of putting a spotlight on the importance of racial justice. An extensive resource for teachers, educators and young people. Excellent.

BrainPOP: free resources for supporting anti-racist education

https://blog.brainpop.com/antiracist-education-free-resources-kids

An extensive set of resources developed by BrainPOP and Black Lives Matter on racial injustice, black history, civil rights and those figures in history who have been leaders and activists for change. This is suitable for use in the classroom or at home.

Bystanders and upstanders

www.holocaust.org.uk/standup

These are two home learning video exercises inviting young people to think about the two choices: to be a Bystander or an Upstander. The videos explore what each of these means. Suitable for KS3 and KS4.

Fight for human rights

www.nobelprize.org/nobel-prize-lessons-theme-the-fight-for-human-rights

A fantastic lesson plan for secondary schools from the Nobel Prize, providing an introduction to human rights and its history. It aims to give students an understanding of human rights in different parts of the world by studying Nobel Laureates' struggles. Excellent.

Football and British values

www.padlet.com/nfmcommunities

The National Football Museum has produced an excellent set of resources looking at the issues and values of football including racism and homophobia. Select Football & British Values.

Genetic engineering: Dolly the sheep

www.nms.ac.uk/explore-our-collections/stories/natural-world/dolly-the-sheep

As the first cloned mammal ever to be created from an adult cell, the birth of Dolly was a historic and significant scientific and ethical moment. Find out more.

Genetic engineering, stem cells and cloning

www.abpischools.org.uk

The Association of the British Pharmaceutical Industry website for schools, children and learning provides a huge number of resources covering science, medicine and treatment of disease. Resources are provided for each age range (5-7, 7-11, 11-14, 14-16 and 16+) with topics listed linked to the curriculum. It provides extensive free, curriculum-related and interactive resources, including animations and diagrams. You will find topics on genetic engineering; stem cells; cloning; and biotechnology, amongst others under PSHE/Citizenship Studies for ages 14-16 and 16-19. Excellent. Well worth a visit.

History of suffrage – Vote 100: The Moving Story toolkit for schools

www.womenslibrary.org.uk/disccover-our-projects/vote-100-the-moving-story/vote-100-toolkit-for-schools

Vote 100: The Moving Story was developed by the Glasgow Women's Library for the 100th anniversary of the Representation of the People Act. The toolkit supports Vote 100 offering activities for research, debate, creative writing and arts to engage 14-16-year-olds. It includes an animated resource to highlight those who campaigned for women to have the right to vote. Excellent.

Human Rights Act

www.amnesty.org.uk/resources/speaker-toolkit-human-rights-act

An excellent toolkit for use with 11-14-year-olds to explore the importance of different human rights, consider who should protect our human rights and how human rights law impacts on our lives in the UK. This is a comprehensive and important learning tool and would be useful beyond its intended age range. All materials have been beautifully illustrated by Chris Riddell. Highly Recommended.

Human rights and activism (for ages 14–19)

www.amnesty.org.uk/activism-resource

A great resource for ages 14 to 19 to learn about human rights under threat and how to be an activist in your community.

Human rights and the civil rights movement

www.nobelprize.org/nobel-prize-lessons-theme-martin-luther-king-jr-and-the-civil-rights-movement

A lesson plan for use in the classroom on Martin Luther King Jr and the civil rights movement from the Nobel Prize.

Human rights and LGBTI

www.amnesty.org.uk/resources/lgbti-rights-activity-pack

This resource enables teachers and parents to explore the human rights of sexual and gender minority groups with children and young people. It includes resources for use with the book *Two Weeks with the Queen* by Morris Gleitzman, which looks at homophobia through the character of Ted. Excellent.

Human rights and solidarity (for ages 7–13)

www.amnesty.org.uk/solidarity-resource

A resource for ages 7 to 13 to learn about human rights and how to show solidarity with key workers in their community.

Magna Carta for the 21st century

https://learning.parliament.uk/en/resources/magna-carta-for-the-21st-century

This is a video on the Magna Carta and the emergence of Parliament. It provides links to the curriculums of the four nations and is suitable for KS2 and KS3.

Martin Luther King in the UK

https://research.ncl.ac.uk/martinlutherking/activities/mlkinuk

A brilliant and extensive downloadable resource designed and produced by Newcastle University. The resource pack has been created to inspire young people to think about the world they live in and how they can help bring about change. It is aimed at 7-16-year-olds (KS2-KS4) and includes lesson plans, handouts, worksheets, music recordings and presentations. Excellent.

National Geographic Kids: Magna Carta

www.natgeokids.com/uk/primary-resource/magna-carta-british-values

Magna Carta downloadable primary resource looking at how and why human rights were originally protected.

Peace – World War 1 Christmas truces

https://research.ncl.ac.uk/martinlutherking/activities/worldwaronechristmastruces

This resource pack has been developed for teachers by Northumbria and Newcastle Universities and the Martin Luther King Peace Committee and provides ideas, lesson plans, handouts and presentations on the remarkable events of the 1914 Christmas Truce. Suitable for 8-14-year-olds. Excellent.

Peace movement: learning resources

www.beatlesstory.com/teacher-resources

This has three interesting resources presenting the background and influences of the peace movement. These are the European Peace Movement; war and its impact; and peace songs. Scroll through the list of resources.

Skin

www.filmeducation.org/skin

Film Education resources to support the film *Skin*, the story of Sandra Laing who was born in 1955 to white Afrikaner parents in South Africa, dark-skinned and with black hair, at the time of Apartheid.

Special times, special stories

www.holocaust.org.uk/special-stories

Three video exercises for primary age children linked to stories shared by three Holocaust survivors.

Stephen Lawrence Day

www.stephenlawrenceday.org/resources

Stephen Lawrence Day is about the part we all play in creating a society in which everyone can flourish and was set up in memory of the murdered school boy Stephen Lawrence. This includes resources linked to the citizenship curriculum, videos and assembly presentations, all to use with children to discuss living in a fairer and just society.

Story explorer

www.amnesty.org.uk/resources/story-explorer-questions-exploring-fiction

Story explorer is a downloadable resource to explore human rights themes in fiction with questions designed to promote discussion and critical thinking.

Sustainable development

www.nobelprize.org/nobel-prize-lessons-sustainable-development

A lesson plan for teachers from the Nobel Prize on sustainable development with four themes - Saving Lives; Feeding Humanity; Protecting the Planet and Connecting the World.

Using fiction to teach human rights

www.amnesty.org.uk/resources/book-and-activities-kill-mockingbird-harper-lee

This is a teaching resource on the human rights at the heart of *To Kill a Mockingbird*. It is a fantastic resource for both teacher and students. It is produced in partnership between Amnesty International and Penguin Random House.

Immigration

The Weight of Water

www.amnesty.org.uk/resources/book-and-activities-weight-water
A downloadable teaching resource to use with the book *The Weight of Water* by Sarah Crossan, which tackles the alienation experienced by young immigrants.

Refugees

My Name is Not Refugee: teachers' toolkit

www.barringtonstoke.co.uk/books/my-name-is-not-refugee-teachers-toolkit
This outstanding resource is designed to build on the questions posed by the book and provides ideas for exploring the themes. It is suitable for KS1 and KS2. Excellent.

No Ballet Shoes in Syria: discussion notes

www.nosycrow.com/resource/no-ballet-shoes-in-syria-discussion-notes
No Ballet Shoes in Syria by Catherine Bruton can be used with children to discuss the refugee crisis and what it means. Suitable for children from 9 years old.

The Bone Sparrow

www.amnesty.org.uk/resources/book-and-activities-bone-sparrow
A downloadable resource for use with the book *The Bone Sparrow* by Zara Fraillon to support children aged 12 and over to explore the issues in the book, in particular looking at refugees, human rights abuse, courage, freedom and protest.

Jewish Museum London: learning resources – refugees

www.jewishmuseum.org.uk/schools/in-the-classroom
This has extensive resources for use in the classroom or at home covering KS1 to A Level. Search by resource type, key stage or by area of study (which includes During War 1939-45; Pre-War 1933-39; Immigration and Migration; and many more). Select Curriculum then Citizenship for a wealth of resources on refugees and their stories.

Refugees and migration

www.redcross.org.uk/get-involved/teaching-resources/refugees-and-migration
A brilliant set of resources from the British Red Cross to explore refugees and migration and to challenge assumptions about migrants, asylum seekers and refugees. Suitable for both primary and secondary. Excellent.

Refugee experiences: primary teaching resources

www.houseofillustration.org.uk/learn/primary-teaching-resources-refugee-experiences

These downloadable resources have been created by the House of Illustration using illustration for teaching and learning about refugee experiences. They were originally created to complement the exhibition *Journeys Dawn: Illustration from the Refugee Crisis*. There are five activities designed for teaching the topic, each dealing with a different aspect of the refugee experience. They are Journeys Drawn (exploring different journeys made by refugees); The Big Picture; Life in a Refugee Camp; Portrait of a Refugee (to explore refugee identity); and Emotional Connections (looking at different refugee experiences). Suitable for KS2 and KS3. Excellent.

Women's rights

Unfinished business: the fight for women's rights in the UK

www.bl.uk/womens-rights

This is an astounding learning and information resource from the British Library. It is packed with information. Excellent.

Also have a look at:

Sisterhood and after

www.bl.uk/sisterhood

Spare Rib

www.bl.uk/spare-rib

C DESIGN AND TECHNOLOGY

Design and Technology brings together a host of 'technologies', which includes graphics, resistant materials (wood, metal, plastics), food technology, textiles and electronics. At school, children will spend a period of time on each during KS2 and KS3 with some opting to study one of the subjects for GCSE or A Level (or the equivalent options within Wales, Scotland and Northern Ireland). For more detail, take a look at the Design and Technology Association (**www.data.org.uk/for-education/curriculum**), which provides a link to the National Curriculum programme of study for Design and Technology. Select Education, then Primary or Secondary. It also links to the National Curriculum for Wales, the curriculum area 'Technologies' for Scotland and the National Curriculum for Science, Technology and Design for Northern Ireland.

The learning resources below provide a range of materials from organisations such as the Design Museum and STEM Learning. There are further additional resources for Food Technology - looking at food production and food nutrition - and Textiles - looking at fabric production and garment design.

Learning resources and activities

Avoncroft Museum: online resources

www.avoncroft.org.uk/online-resources

Avoncroft Museum is home to 30 historic buildings. It has an interesting set of downloadable resources for four different buildings: a 15th century town house; a 1946 prefab; a 1790 windmill; and a 1576 Tudor timber framed building. An unusual learning resource that includes templates to create a model of each building and could be incorporated into design topics.

Brand evolution: learning resource

www.museumofbrands.com/online-resources

A useful resource looking at brand design for GCSE students from the Museum of Brands.

The Design Museum

www.designmuseum.org/the-design-museum-campus/schoolsandcolleges

This has an excellent collection of online lesson plans and downloadable PDF design activities, including resources for GCSE and above. All aim to make students consider related design projects and to inspire creativity. They include a kitchen re-design; re-using rubbish; and environmentally friendly packaging, amongst others.

National Geographic Kids: Design and Technology resources

www.natgeokids.com/uk/teacher-category/technology

A selection of downloadable resources for KS2 on significant design and technological developments that have shaped our world.

Plastics: GCSE learning resources

www.modip.ac.uk/engagement

Select Learning Resources, then GCSE Learning Resources. These downloadable resources from the Museum of Design in Plastics support GCSE Design and Technology knowledge and understanding relating specifically to plastic materials. Excellent.

Primary teaching ideas: DT

www.teachingideas.co.uk/subjects/dt

KS1 and KS2 downloadable teaching ideas, resources and activities for Design and Technology. Excellent.

STEM Learning: GCSE Design and Technology resources

www.stem.org.uk/gcse-design-and-technology-resources

This has downloadable resources for GCSE Design and Technology covering designing; materials; manufacturing; production techniques and electronic systems; emerging technologies; and many more. A fantastic resource.

Costume

Victoria and Albert Museum: costume

www.vam.ac.uk/collections/costume

The Victoria and Albert Museum has over 3,500 stage costumes and accessories from the 18th century onwards that can be explored online.

Fashion

The roaring twenties: how the jazz age changed fashion

www.museumcrush.org/the-roaring-twenties-how-the-jazz-age-changed-fashion

The Keeper of Costume at Chertsey Museum explains how fashion was transformed during the 1920s. Includes links to further information about the influence of fashion in a historical context.

Victoria and Albert Museum Fashion Resource

www.vam.ac.uk/info/teachers-resources-for-secondary-schools-and-colleges

Select Fashion and Fashion and Textiles: State of Early Modern Undress. These resources are aimed at KS3, KS4 and KS5 and use the collection to explore fashion and costume. The latter aims to develop an understanding of garment construction and give pointers to students for design projects. This would be useful as a starting point for textile students and for historical context.

Food technology

British Nutrition Foundation: food – a fact of life

www.foodafactoflife.org.uk

This provides a huge range of useful teaching resources and videos to support teaching and learning about food with children and young people from 3 to 16 years. They have been developed to be used by teachers to encourage an interest in food as well as to support the curriculum. It covers healthy eating; cooking; food production and farming; food science; consumer awareness; where food comes from; and food commodities. The section on where food comes from covers food processing, product development and food packaging, along with genetic modification and biotechnology. It has excellent downloadable learning resources. In addition, there is a section for remote learning, which has a wealth of STEM activities and resources to support learning at home. The activities are even divided into those that take a small amount of time and those that are more complicated. Excellent.

Chocolate inventing: learning resource

www.museumofbrands.com/online-resources

A useful resource looking at chocolate confectionary design for KS1, KS2 and KS3 from the Museum of Brands.

Fab Flour

www.fabflour.co.uk/fab-bread

This provides information on flour - its production, types of flour and the milling industry, along with the role of flour and bread in the UK diet. It has some colourful infographics to support the information.

Food and diet

www.abpischools.org.uk/topic/balanced-diet/1/1

A learning resource from the Association of the British Pharmaceutical Industry to support young people in understanding the need for a balanced diet.

Growing food

www.chatsworth.org/your-visit/learning/learning-resources/resources-for-ages-5-7

Learn about where our food comes from and what fruit and vegetables need to help them grow. This is an outline resource developed for use at home. It looks at what children can find in the kitchen, garden or allotment, discusses what plants need to grow, identifies which parts of different food-producing plants can be eaten and discusses seasonality and plant structure. It is aimed at KS1 and KS2, however it offers a template for adapting for KS3 and could equally be used in the classroom. Select Growing Food.

STEM Learning: GCSE food preparation and nutrition

www.stem.org.uk/gcse-food-preparation

This covers food preparation; food nutrition and health; food science; food safety; and more.

Textiles

National Wool Museum: from fleece to fabric

www.museum.wales/wool/learning/resources

A short resource showing the stages of producing fabric from fleece. Select From Fleece to Fabric.

The Quilters' Guild: learning resources

www.quiltmuseum.org.uk/learning-centre/adult-community-learners

This downloadable learning resource is aimed at teachers and educators. It includes information on the history of quilting and patchwork, interviews with quilt artists, lesson plans, worksheets and images. There is also a Tips and Techniques section, which has video clips and guides to different textile techniques. A great resource for textile students looking for design ideas and inspiration from the past.

Talking textiles

www.childrensuniversity.manchester.ac.uk/learning-activities/art-design/talking-textiles/introduction

A fantastic learning resource from the Children's University in Manchester and the Whitworth Art Gallery, part of Manchester University. This has a series of modules on aspects of finding out about textiles. These include: what are textiles?; how are textiles made?; how are textiles decorated?; patterns and textiles; world costumes; and how do textiles talk - how we can learn the history of the past from textiles. The format and structure are great, taking the student through the subject one step at a time. Suitable for KS2, KS3 and KS4 and anyone who has an interest in textiles and design. Excellent.

Tapestry arts

www.cadw.gov.wales/learn/education/teaching-resources/tapestry-arts

A short resource from CADW looking at textile art. It includes some good ideas for developing design.

Tartan and kilts

www.visitscotland.com/about/uniquely-scottish/kilts-tartan

Find out about the tartan fabric unique to Scotland. This includes a link to the Scottish Register of Tartans which includes thousands of designs.

Textile archive colouring sheets

www.braintreemuseum.co.uk/online-educational-resources

An interesting resource for design research. Select from the various textile colouring sheets available.

Textiles: secondary resources

www.nms.ac.uk/explore-our-collections/resources/for-teachers-secondary-resources

Select Fashion to explore 30 objects from the world of fashion through high quality 360° images and information on topics such as design, craft skills and the social and cultural background to each piece. Suitable for BGE Art & Design & Senior Phase Art & Design, GCSE and A Level.

Unravelling the thread: the story of cotton

https://schools.fairtrade.org.uk/resource/unravelling-the-thread

This film from Fairtrade helps young people understand the impact of fast fashion. It has related activities to download. Suitable for age 11–14 years.

Worcester embroidery peacock

www.museumsworcestershire.org.uk/collections/activities

Downloadable instructions and design template for re-creating the peacock from the Bromgrove Guild's stained glass window. Select Beautiful Embroidery Peacock.

DINOSAURS

See also: Famous People - Mary Anning

Dinosaurs remain as popular as ever with younger children. As well as the resources below, there will be a plethora of dinosaur books available at your local library. In this section, you will find dinosaur facts, fossil facts and fun activities to support learning.

Information

Dinosaur factsheet

www.geolsoc.org.uk/factsheets

The Geological Society produces a list of factsheets. Select Dinosaurs for a downloadable and colourful factsheet.

Dinosaurs: books

www.lovemybooks.co.uk/dinosaurs

For books about dinosaurs, along with activities and links to find out more.

Natural History Museum: everything you've always wanted to know about dinosaurs

www.nhm.ac.uk/events/dinosaur-activities-for-families.html

A brilliant set of resources and fun activities on dinosaurs, including the Dino Directory giving facts, figures and images for over 300 dinosaurs. Excellent.

Learning resources and activities

The Big Jurassic: primary classroom resources

www.jurassiccoast.org/what-is-the-jurassic-coast/things-to-do/jurassic-coast-teachers-resources

A downloadable resource to support the teaching of rocks, fossils and evolution developed by the Primary Science Teaching Trust in conjunction with the Jurassic Coast Trust. It has a downloadable book that brings together resources and information to show teachers and educators how they can use their local environments to inspire interest in the UK's geological history. The activity pack provides images, worksheets and activity instructions for children aged 3-7 and 7-11. In addition, there are further resources available to download on the theme of the Jurassic Coast, plus links to factsheets from the Geological Society. Excellent.

Dinosaur colouring pages

www.thedinosaurmuseum.com/colouring-pages

Downloadable and printable colouring pages.

Dinosaur crafts to make

www.life.org.uk/downloadable-resources

Select Create a Flapping Pterosaur, Build-a-Bone Dino or Make a Snapping Dinosaur. It also includes a good set of dinosaur colouring and activity sheets.

Dinosaur Detectives e-book

www.museum.wales/cardiff/learning/resources

A downloadable e-book or PDF from Cardiff Museum to discover facts about dinosaurs. Select E-book - Dinosaur Detectives. Excellent.

Dinosaurs – learning with Spike at home

https://museum.maidstone.gov.uk/learn/learning-with-spike-at-home

Select School History Themes - Dinosaurs (KS1) for an info-activity download from Maidstone Museum.

Ely Museum: prehistoric creatures

www.elymuseum.org.uk/uncategorised/museumfromhome-prehistoric-creatures

Looks at the process of fossilisation with downloadable related crafts.

Make a dinosaur activity

www.lymeregismuseum.co.uk/make-and-do

Excellent downloadable activities to make an ammonite, ichthyosaur, plesiosaur or dimorphodon. Or make a dinosaur model or a model of fossil hunter Mary Anning using clay.

Oxford University Museum of Natural History: fossils

www.oum.ox.ac.uk/thezone/fossils

Designed for younger children to find facts and information about fossils.

C DRAMA AND THEATRE STUDIES (INCLUDING PERFORMING ARTS)

See also: English – English literature

There are a number of learning resources from the National Theatre, the Royal Opera House and the Royal Shakespeare Company looking at the stage and plays. There is also a wealth of resources on Shakespeare that will be useful for English Literature too. In addition, theatre and drama is about storytelling so activities such as making a model theatre are great ways to engage a child's imagination and deliver performance poetry, storytelling, puppetry or playwriting.

Information

The story of theatre

www.vam.ac.uk/articles/the-story-of-theatre

An excellent resource from the Victoria and Albert Museum charting the history of theatre in Britain from the middle ages to the present day.

Learning resources and activities

A trip to the theatre

www.dur.ac.uk/4schools/learningonline/primaryonline/theatre

Recreate plays at home with these simplified playscripts based on original Ancient Greek plays. A great way to have fun, learn about Ancient Greece and storytelling through drama. Excellent.

Build your own puppet theatre

www.royalalberthall.com/about-the-hall/news/2020/april/build-your-own-royal-albert-hall-puppet-theatre

Downloadable templates to create the Royal Albert Hall with puppet characters from the archives.

Create a 3D theatre Inspired by Edgar Degas

www.courtauld.ac.uk/learn/family-activities/create-a-3d-theatre

A downloadable resource from the Courtauld to create a model theatre inspired by Edgar Degas and his ballet dancers.

Make a shadow theatre

www.lakesidearts.org.uk/take-part-learn/inwithlakeside/Little-Angel-Theatre-Shadow-Theatre.html

A story using shadow puppets from Little Angel Theatre, with a downloadable activity from Lakeside Arts (part of the University of Nottingham) to make a shadow theatre. Suitable for 5-11-year-olds.

National Theatre: resource packs

www.nationaltheatre.org.uk/content/resource-packs-list

The National Theatre has downloadable resource packs and rehearsal diaries for a significant number of productions and plays staged by the theatre. They are suitable for secondary pupils and teachers, along with parents supporting learning at home. Plays include *Macbeth*, *Midsummer Night's Dream* and *His Dark Materials*, to name but a few. In addition, it has resources within the Learn at Home section. These include How We Made It, which offers an insight into theatre-making at the National Theatre with an extensive collection of videos and audio recorded talks and events. Plus, How You Can Make It offers online YouTube tutorials on the art of theatre, with the chance to learn theatre-making skills from puppetry to playwriting.

Royal Opera House: learning resources

https://learning-platform.roh.org.uk

The Royal Opera House Learning Platform has cross-curricular creative learning activities for children and young people linked to the National Curriculum for Dance, Music and Art & Design. The content of the learning platform has been written for and by teachers and offers a wonderful set of creative education resources for teachers, educators and young people from KS1 onwards. In addition, it provides a set of lesson plans on opera and dramatic singing aimed primarily at younger children up to 11 years. There are also some simple activities to do at home. Select Create & Learn.

Royal Shakespeare Company

www.rsc.org.uk/education

A wealth of information and resources, including live lessons and teaching resources for use within the classroom or at home. By selecting Teacher Resources, you can specify the play, the type of resource and the key stage required. Excellent.

Victoria and Albert Museum: theatre and performance resource

www.vam.ac.uk/info/learn

These resources are linked to a museum visit, however there are elements of the resources that can be extracted and re-purposed for learning at home and in the classroom. Includes some useful images. Worth a look.

Shakespeare and his plays

Leather in Shakespeare

www.nationalleathercollection.org/leather-in-shakespeare-online

An online exhibition resource from the National Leather Collection detailing the references to leather items in Shakespeare's plays. An interesting resource looking at life in Shakespearian times and explaining some of the references made to the leather objects.

Royal Shakespeare Company: homework help

www.rsc.org.uk/education/about-rsc-education/home-learning-with-the-rsc/homework-help

Actors and directors have answered questions from students, which are arranged by topics including questions about Acting and Directing; Shakespeare Tragedies; Comedies; and Histories. Although it does require scrolling through the questions, the answers are very informative and worth the effort.

Shakespeare activity toolkits

www.rsc.org.uk/education/about-rsc-education/home-learning-with-the-rsc/activity-toolkits

The Royal Shakespeare Company has extensive downloadable toolkits to support students, families and teachers in learning about Shakespeare. Toolkits are available for *Macbeth*, *Romeo and Juliet*, *Hamlet*, *The Merchant of Venice*, *Othello* and *Much Ado About Nothing*.

Shakespeare: learning resources

www.shakespeare.org.uk/education/teaching-resources

An extensive range of downloadable teaching resources for school or home learning. It includes Shakespeare's language, individual Shakespeare plays and historical context, which can be selected by teaching level and by resource type. Excellent. Use also: **www.shakespeare.org.uk/education/home-learning**

Shakespeare learning zone

www.rsc.org.uk/shakespeare-learning-zone

The Shakespeare learning zone from the Royal Shakespeare Company is a fantastic resource providing a wealth of information about Shakespeare's plays. It has key facts, key scenes, pictures from past productions, videos of actors and directors working on and performing the plays and information on the main characters and how they relate to each other. Simply select a play from the list. Excellent.

Shakespeare's plays (RSC)

www.rsc.org.uk/shakespeares-plays

Find plot synopses, archive material, production photos and video content for all Shakespeare's plays. Packed with information from the Royal Shakespeare Company. Excellent.

Shakespeare's plays (Shakespeare's Globe theatre)

https://teach.shakespearesglobe.com

Absolutely fantastic learning resource providing resources to teach Shakespeare by play, theme, language and character. It has lesson plans and exam revision guides along with exclusive content. Designed for use in the classroom or at home with KS3, KS4 and KS5.

Shakespeare for primary school children

www.shakespearesglobe.com/learn/playground

Provides an introduction to Shakespeare for children from 5-11 years.

Shakespeare teaching resources

www.shakespearesglobe.com/learn/teaching-resources/#resources

Shakespeare's Globe theatre offers an outstanding set of teaching resources for all ages and levels and for use by schools or for learning at home. It includes a dedicated teaching website, resources from previous productions, a 360° virtual tour of the Globe Theatre, productions to stream in the classroom and textbooks for classroom study. Excellent.

Shakespeare's world

www.shakespearesglobe.com/discover/shakespeares-world

Packed with facts and information to discover the world that Shakespeare lived in. Excellent.

Shakespedia

www.shakespeare.org.uk/explore-shakespeare/shakespedia

Find out about the life and works of William Shakespeare.

DRUGS, ALCOHOL AND SMOKING

See also: PSHE (Personal, Social, Health and Economic Education)

Although drug, smoking and alcohol education and awareness is part of the PSHE curriculum, it is by no means confined to classroom learning. There are many good resources available from organisations such as Childline to share and discuss with children and young people at home.

Information

Action on Smoking and Health: factsheets

www.ash.org.uk/fact-sheets

Excellent set of factsheets on smoking, the risks to health and the tobacco industry.

Alcohol and young people

www.teachingideas.co.uk/healthy-lifestyles/alcohol-and-young-people

A very useful report from Drinkaware to use with KS3 pupils when discussing alcohol issues.

Drugs and alcohol (young people)

www.healthtalk.org/drugs-and-alcohol/overview

This has interviews with 33 young people about their experiences of and opinion on recreational drugs and alcohol. It looks at the issues surrounding why young people use drugs and alcohol. Useful for discussions. Also provides signposting to other organisations for help and information.

FRANK

www.talktofrank.com

This is designed for young people and has a comprehensive A–Z list of drugs. For each, it gives an explanation of what the drug is, slang or street names, the effects, the chances of getting hooked, the law, the appearance and use, the cost, purity and risks. It also signposts young people to where they can get help or simply chat. Excellent.

Know the Score

www.knowthescore.info

An excellent site, packed with information and advice on drugs in Scotland. It has an A–Z list of drugs. Excellent.

Release

www.release.org.uk

This provides a list of drugs with information on the chemistry, history and the risks associated with a drug.

Talking about drugs and alcohol

www.nspcc.org.uk/keeping-children-safe/talking-drugs-alcohol
The NSPCC offers information and advice to help parents talk to children and young people about the risks of alcohol and taking drugs.

Young people and smoking

www.ash.org.uk/information-and-resources/fact-sheets/young-people-and-smoking
A factsheet on the changing attitudes to smoking by young people.

Learning resources and activities

Action on Smoking and Health: young people and tobacco

www.ash.org.uk/category/information-and-resources
This is packed with information for PSHE discussions on young people and tobacco.

Childline: drugs, alcohol and smoking

www.childline.org.uk/info-advice/you-your-body/drugs-alcohol-smoking
This has fantastic resources and information on drug and alcohol use and smoking.

Drugs and their effects

www.teachingideas.co.uk/pshe/drugs-and-their-effects
A downloadable short resource to help children learn about different drugs and the effect on the body.

C ENGLISH (LITERACY) AND ENGLISH LITERATURE

See also: Drama and Theatre Studies; Books, reading and stories

There is no shortage of resources for help with the English language, however this proliferation can often make it difficult to find the right materials. English in itself is a huge subject area and not simply a collection of over one million words. It is ever evolving, with new words added to its dictionary every year and new literature being created by authors, poets, playwrights and all manner of wordsmiths on a daily basis. The aim of this section is to inspire children and young people with resources that stimulate creativity and engage the imagination as well as provide access to understanding the principles of the English language.

The areas covered are: English Grammar; English Language and Literacy for Primary; English Language and Literacy for Secondary; Writing Skills for Primary; Writing Skills for Secondary; English Literature; Authors and their Books; Plays; Poetry and Comics. Within each, there are learning resources from a variety of sources. Both the Writing Skills and the Poetry sections bring together creative writing activities from an eclectic mix of museums, galleries and organisations and provide a wide range of writing ideas and styles to use either at home or within the classroom - from letter writing as an evacuee to diary writing as a passenger on the SS Great Britain, from Haiku poetry to Words That Burn.

Authors and their books

A Christmas Carol Charles Dickens

www2.bfi.org.uk/victorian-masculinity

This uses silent film to enhance the study of Victorian literature for KS3 and KS4. The lesson plans and films offer context for studying *A Christmas Carol* by Charles Dickens.

Barrington Stoke: A Christmas Carol resources

www.barringtonstoke.co.uk/books/a-christmas-carol-resources

These resources have been designed to guide students through Charles Dickens' *A Christmas Carol*. It includes a synopsis of the book, key characters, themes and scenes, providing quotes for each of these key areas. Excellent.

Also available:

Barrington Stoke: Of Mice and Men resources

www.barringtonstoke.co.uk/books/of-mice-and-men-resources

Barrington Stoke: The Strange Case of Dr Jekyll and Mr Hyde resources

www.barringtonstoke.co.uk/books/the-strange-case-of-dr-jekyll-and-mr-hyde-resources

Jane Austen: British Library Discovering Literature

www.bl.uk/people/jane-austen

A host of resources for students and teachers, including essays and digitised images of primary sources.

Jane Austen: learning resources

www.janeaustens.house/learn/learning-resources

This has learning resources designed for use by teachers and home-schooling parents to help teach Austen effectively. It includes *Jane Austen: Life and Times - Background Information for Teachers of KS1 & KS2* and *The World That Jane Austen Presents for KS3-KS5*. In addition, it has the Jane Austen Glossary, which is a list of some unfamiliar words pupils might come across when studying Jane Austen, and a Jane Austen Timeline for KS3-KS5. Excellent.

Screen Online

www.screenonline.org.uk

Select Education for access to films and television titles from 1890 to 2014. Access the Lesson Bank for links to curriculum covering English, with film and lesson plans for *Persuasion*; *Pride and Prejudice*; *Great Expectations* and *Oliver Twist*. This has some amazing films and documentaries with detailed lesson plans. Fantastic to use in the classroom or for learning at home. Excellent.

The Traditional Teacher: English literature

www.thetraditionalteacher.wordpress.com/english-resources

This has a wealth of KS3 resources and study guides for English literature texts including *Macbeth*; *A Christmas Carol*; *Romeo and Juliet*; *The Strange Case of Dr Jekyll and Mr Hyde*; *An Inspector Calls*; and *Animal Farm*. It includes various curriculum poetry looking at texts and themes. Excellent.

To Kill a Mockingbird: Using Fiction to teach Human Rights

www.amnesty.org.uk/resources/book-and-activities-kill-mockingbird-harper-lee

This is a teaching resource on the human rights at the heart of *To Kill a Mockingbird*. It is a fantastic resource for both teachers and students. It is produced in partnership between Amnesty International and Penguin Random House.

William Golding

www.william-golding.co.uk

This provides some information on the books of William Golding, including *Lord of the Flies*.

World War 1: Tolkien's experiences

www.britishlegion.org.uk/get-involved/remembrance/teaching-remembrance/ks4-lesson-plans

An excellent resource to consider how Tolkien's experiences influenced his writing.

Comics

Comics in the curriculum

www.houseofillustration.org.uk/learn/secondary-teaching-resources-comics-in-the-curriculum

This is a collection of resources designed to use the study of drawing and comics as a means to develop core KS3 English skills, including critical analysis and descriptive language techniques. Excellent.

DIY comics

www.sevenstories.org.uk/learning/books-and-resources/diy-comics

Three downloadable resources for children to make their own comics.

English grammar

BBC Bitesize: English

www.bbc.co.uk/bitesize/learn

Select either Primary, Secondary or Post 16. Then select the specific key stage relevant to England, Northern Ireland, Scotland or Wales, then select English. For GCSE, select the exam board relevant to your school. Topics for English include Analysing Fiction; Analysing Non-Fiction; Comparing Texts; Writing; Spelling; Punctuation and Grammar; and Spoken Language. Packed with information, worksheets and tests. Excellent.

National Geographic Kids: English

www.natgeokids.com/uk/teacher-category/english

This covers comprehension; grammar and punctuation; phonics; reading; spelling; and writing.

Oxford University Press: free English resources

https://global.oup.com/education/dictionaries/?region=uk

This has a wealth of resources for English language skills and is packed with activity sheets. Suitable for KS1 to KS3. Select free dictionary and worksheets downloads. Excellent.

Skillswise: spelling

www.bbc.co.uk/teach/skillswise/spelling/z6c6d6f

This is an excellent site to improve spelling and to test spelling knowledge. It includes downloadable factsheets and worksheets.

English language and literacy for primary

Centre for Literacy in Primary Education (CLPE): free resources

www.clpe.org.uk/clpe/free-resources

The Centre for Literacy in Primary Education (CLPE) is a charity working with all those involved in teaching literacy in primary schools. The free resources are available to all, which includes teachers, educators and parents. They cover literacy, poetry and booklists and provide a wealth of material, lesson plans and activities to support literacy, creative writing and poetry. Excellent.

Oxford Owl for Home: English

https://home.oxfordowl.co.uk/english

A wonderful and extensive learning resource from Oxford University Press for children from 5 to 11 years, including some downloadable worksheets. It covers Spelling; Grammar and Punctuation; Vocabulary; Handwriting and Writing. It also includes a grammar and literacy glossary to help parents understand or remember common English terms and phrases, which is worth looking at and is very useful. It also provides information to parents as to what children will be learning at each year of school.

Oxford Owl for Home: reading

https://home.oxfordowl.co.uk/reading

A wonderful and extensive learning resource from Oxford University Press for children from 5 to 11 years, including a phonics guide and tips on comprehension. In addition, Oxford Owl offers a free eBook library for children aged 3–11. It includes Oxford's primary school brands, such as Oxford Reading Tree and Read Write Inc, as well as stories from Read with Oxford. The eBook service simply requires registration and use of a computer, laptop or tablet.

Learning resources and activities

Down's Syndrome Association: nursery rhymes

www.downs-syndrome.org.uk/download-package/communications-series-nursery-rhymes

A set of nursery rhyme prompts to use with children with learning difficulties. There are also Early Years Communication Cards: **www.downs-syndrome.org.uk/download-package/communications-series-early-vocab-pictures-and-words**

See also: **www.downs-syndrome.org.uk/download-package/communication-series-listening-cards**

Fairy tales

www.nls.uk/learning-zone/literature-and-language/themes-in-focus/fairy-tales

This learning resource from the National Library of Scotland is for primary age children P3-P7 (KS1 and KS2). It uses sources from the National Library to highlight different elements of fairy tales - the different character types and the fairy tale settings. The activity is mapped to the Curriculum for Excellence in Scotland but can equally be used in English, Welsh and Northern Irish schools. It includes discussion, lesson materials and downloadable activities. Excellent.

Incredible Journeys

www.storymuseum.org.uk/schools-groups/learning-resources

Incredible Journeys is a learning resource created by the Story Museum, Oxford, to support World War 1 learning. It tells the stories of World War 1 using animals from all round the world. There are downloadable lesson packs for each story providing background context and teaching ideas to use either at home or in the classroom. Suitable for KS2 and KS3. Excellent.

Literacy Shed

www.literacyshedplus.com/en-gb/browse/free-resources

A wealth of resources available to download covering KS1 and KS2 literacy. Excellent.

Primary school teaching ideas

www.teachingideas.co.uk

Select English. This is brilliant as a teaching and learning resource for both teachers and parents with children learning at home. Well worth a visit.

Traditional tales

www.teachingideas.co.uk/themes/traditional-tales

Teaching ideas and resources using traditional tales for KS1 and KS2. Resources can be downloaded and are useful either in the classroom or at home. Excellent.

Words: learning resources

www.childrensuniversity.manchester.ac.uk/learning-activities/languages/words/introduction

A fantastic learning resource from the Children's University in Manchester and the Linguistics department of Manchester University. It looks at language, exploring different languages and providing modules on understanding the English language. Suitable for KS2.

World War 1 and World War 2: literacy teaching resources

www.dur.ac.uk/4schools/learningonline/primaryonline

Download literacy worksheets looking at archival material from the two World Wars.

English language and literacy for secondary

British Library: teaching resources for English language

www.bl.uk/teaching-resources?nativelanguage=english

A huge amount of teaching resources linked to the English language curriculum for ages 11 - 14, 14 - 16 and 16 - 18, covering topics such as crime and punishment and Windrush stories. There are also links to British Library online resources.

English Mastery: KS3 resources

www.arkcurriculumplus.org.uk/home-learning/ks3-resources

This has downloadable resource packs for KS3 English writing and poetry.

Grammar Slammer

www.englishplus.com/grammar/index.htm

This provides extensive information on English grammar.

National Association for the Teaching of English: home learning resources

www.nate.org.uk/home-learning

The National Association for the Teaching of English (NATE) provides a range of teaching resources to support parents, teachers and young people. They include GCSE English Literature Revision, Shakespeare Resources, Creative Persuasion, Grammar for Writing and 19th Century Novels.

Skillswise: English

www.bbc.co.uk/teach/skillswise/english/zjg4scw

Great for video and downloadable worksheets for grammar, punctuation, writing, reading, speaking and listening. It is aimed at adults however the worksheets are suitable for 11 - 18-year-olds.

English literature

British Library: teaching resources for English literature

www.bl.uk/teaching-resources?teachingsubjects=english-literature

A huge selection of teaching resources for English literature linked to the curriculum. It includes: *A Christmas Carol*; *A Midsummer Night's Dream*; *An Inspector Calls*; *Emma*; *Persuasion*; *Pride and Prejudice*; *Jane Eyre*; *Wuthering Heights*; *Great Expectations*; *Oliver Twist*; *Hard Times*; *Frankenstein*; *Animal Farm*; *A Room with a View*; *Hamlet*; *Tess of the d'Urbervilles*; *Macbeth*; *The Strange Case of Dr Jekyll and Mr Hyde*; *Anthem for Doomed Youth*; and more. Excellent.

GCSE English Literature revision cards

www.literacytrust.org.uk/resources/gcse-english-literature-revision-cards

This series of revision materials is designed to support students to understand key themes and characters within GCSE English Literature set texts. For each text, the important quotes and brief analysis is included. These materials have been developed in collaboration with Read Manchester Campaign. Texts covered are: *A Christmas Carol*; *An Inspector Calls*; *DNA* by Dennis Kelly; *Frankenstein*; *Macbeth*; *Pigeon English* by Stephen Kelman; *Romeo and Juliet*; and *The Strange Case of Dr Jekyll and Mr Hyde*.

National Library of Scotland: learning resources

www.nls.uk/learning-zone/literature-and-language

This covers a range of resources on Scottish writers and literature, including John Buchan's *The Thirty-Nine Steps*.

Plays

An Inspector Calls

www.vam.ac.uk/info/teachers-resources-for-secondary-schools-and-colleges

Scroll down and select An Inspector Calls under the heading Performing Art, Media and English. Although this resource is linked to a visit to the Victoria and Albert Museum, it offers some interesting links to find out more about the play that are well worth looking at.

Macbeth: a teachers toolkit

www.bl.uk/teaching-resources/discovering-literature-teachers-toolkit-macbeth

This offers a wealth of ideas and resources to teach the play, its context and criticism. Resources can be downloaded and have been written by the English and Media Centre and the British Learning Team.

Poetry

Bloomsbury Children's Publishing: poetry activity pack

www.bloomsbury.com/uk/superpage/activity-packs

An excellent resource from Bloomsbury Children's Publishing for exploring poetry. Select from Activity Packs 9–11 years. Highly recommended for classroom use or at home.

Centre for Literacy in Primary Education (CLPE): poetry resources

www.clpe.org.uk/clpe/free-resources

The CLPE is a charity working with all those involved in teaching literacy in primary schools. The free resources are available to all, which includes teachers, educators and parents. There are a number of fantastic poetry resources available. Select National Poetry Day Teaching Resources or Free Poet Videos and Teaching Plans.

Children's Poetry Archive

www.childrenspoetryarchive.org

Lots of poems to listen to and read.

Fun poetry

www.fizzyfunnyfuzzy.com

The home of funny poetry with poet Gareth Lancaster.

Haiku poetry

www.chesterfield.gov.uk/explore-chesterfield/museum/more-from-your-museum/things-to-do/activities.aspx

Find out what a haiku is and then create your own. It has a fantastic set of words denoting the number of syllables in each. Excellent.

How to make poetry stories

www.scottishbooktrust.com/learning-resources/how-to-make-poetry-stones

Poetry stones is an activity that can be used in the classroom or at home and is a creative way to generate ideas for poetry writing. It is suitable for 6-16-year-olds.

John Foster – Children's Poet

www.johnfosterchildrenspoet.co.uk

This is a fun site for children to explore poetry.

Mulga Bill's Cycling Journey

www.bikeability.org.uk/tools-for-schools/learning-resources

Scroll down to KS2 English. This is a quirky learning resource using poetry to develop reading, comprehension, speaking and listening skills.

National Coal Mining Museum: poetry resource

www.ncm.org.uk/learning/learning-resources/art-and-music

This has resources exploring coal mining through folk arts and poetry.

National Poetry Day

www.nationalpoetryday.co.uk

Packed with resources, poetry recommendations and poems. A must for all year around not just for National Poetry Day (the first Thursday in October each year). Excellent.

Performance poetry: learning activities

www.scottishbooktrust.com/learning-resources/performance-poetry-learning-activities

This resource is for exploring spoken word artists and performance poetry with young people. It is suitable for 12-18-year-olds.

Picture the Poet

www.npg.org.uk/whatson/picturethepoet/learn/resources

This is an excellent teacher resource to creatively look at poetry. It is in partnership with the National Portrait Gallery, the National Literacy Trust and Apples and Snakes, the organisation for poetry, and looks at living British poets. There are activities to encourage curiosity about poems and to play with language. In addition, there are audio and video recordings to listen to and watch poetry readings and interviews with the poets included in Picture the Poet. It is aimed at KS2 and KS3. Excellent.

Poetry at the Crags: poetry activities

www.creswell-crags.org.uk/education/crags-at-home-resources

Four downloadable poetry activities created by Creswell Crags that cover four different styles of poetry. Well worth a look.

The Poetry Foundation

www.poetryfoundation.org/learn

A fantastic resource with a section for children and resources for parents. Includes poems and videos for children from 0 to 12 years and a section for teens, which has poems and articles about poetry for young people from 13 to 18 years. It is worth exploring the whole site as there is so much to discover. Excellent.

Poetry resources to inspire creativity

www.museumoflondon.org.uk/schools/learning-resources

Select Secondary then select Poetry Resources. Aimed at KS3 and KS4, this uses objects from the Museum of London to inspire poetry. The resource offers lots of quotes, definitions and activities related to poetry and would be useful for teachers creating resources of their own.

The Poetry Society

www.poetrysociety.org.uk/education/learning-from-home

Hundreds of resources for teachers, children, young people and parents from KS1 to further education. The resources have been written by poets and teachers to spark creativity and a love for poetry writing and reading. Resources can be selected by theme, technique and key stage. In addition, explore the many other resources and material offered by the Poetry Society. Fantastic.

The Poetry Zone

www.poetryzone.co.uk

Great for teachers and parents teaching poetry and for children, young people, teachers and parents looking for poems and wanting to find out about poets.

Pollinators and poetry

www.buglife.org.uk/get-involved/children-and-schools/b-lines-school-pack

A great original resource for children to explore the wonders of the insect world through poetry.

Remembrance through poetry: KS1

www.britishlegion.org.uk/get-involved/remembrance/teaching-remembrance/key-stage-1

This resource from the Royal British Legion has a downloadable powerpoint to use a poem and poetry reading by poet Joseph Coelho.

Remembrance through poetry: KS2

www.britishlegion.org.uk/get-involved/remembrance/teaching-remembrance/ks2-lesson-plans

This resource from the Royal British Legion has a downloadable powerpoint to use a poem and poetry reading by poet Laura Mucha.

Rhyme Zone

www.rhymezone.com

Type in a word and find out dozens of rhyming words. Wonderful for budding poets and great fun too.

Scottish Poetry Library: learning resources

www.scottishpoetrylibrary.org.uk/learning

Packed with learning and teaching resources to explore poetry. It includes the option to select by language and age group.

Words That Burn

www.amnesty.org.uk/resources/download-words-burn-resources

A fantastic resource to enable young people to explore human rights and self-expression through poetry. It is produced by Amnesty International and The Poetry Hour. It is an extensive resource covering 10 sessions for pupils from 11 years onwards. Each session covers a theme to show the power of poetry and to explore different poets, along with developing styles. It is a brilliant resource to use in the classroom or for home learning. Packed with information and poems to discover from a host of poets and accompanied by downloads and videos. Excellent.

Poets

Dylan Thomas literacy resource pack

www.cadw.gov.wales/learn/education/teaching-resources/key-stage-2-education-packs

Select Dylan Thomas Literacy Resource Pack. Although developed for use at

Laugharne Castle, the resources, including lesson plans and supporting materials, are so extensive that those studying or teaching Dylan Thomas will find a wealth of learning ideas.

Introducing and exploring poetry

www.scottishbooktrust.com/learning-resources/introducing-poetry-in-the-classroom
This resource explores poems by Michael Rosen, Joseph Coelho, Joshua Seigal and James Carter. It includes poetry activities and a poetry toolkit, along with how to create a poetry friendly classroom - or, of course, a poetry friendly home. Suitable for 6-11-year-olds. Excellent.

Michael Rosen: learning activities

www.scottishbooktrust.com/learning-resources/michael-rosen-activity-pack
This learning resource has been created to support the use of Michael Rosen's poetry in class. Excellent.

Writing skills for primary

Brontë children: make your own little book

www.bronte.org.uk/learning/childrenscrafts/little-book
Facsimile manuscript to create your own miniature 'Brontë' style book.

Brunel's SS Great Britain: creative writing diary entry

www.ssgreatbritain.org/brunel-institute/learning/stuff-do-home/creative-writing
This has writing activities inspired by the journey of SS Great Britain. Links to:

Global stories: the people of SS Great Britain

This is a huge database of passengers and crew of the SS Great Britain. It charts the origin and journey of over 30,000 of the ship's inhabitants and has passenger diaries. Access online at **www.ssgreatbritain.org/global-stories** to find out stories of passengers and life on board. A fascinating creative writing project to enjoy in the classroom or at home, with links to history and geography.

Creative writing for upper primary

www.scottishbooktrust.com/learning-resources/creative-writing-activities-for-upper-primary
The activities in this resource are designed to use a favourite author as a starting point for individual, paired and group work. Suitable for 6-11 years.

Creative writing: composition

www.culturestreet.org.uk/lesson.php?id=75
Culture Street provides a writing skills lesson plan for KS2 English composition. It suggests writing and discussion activities all available to download.

Creative writing: if buildings could talk

www.courtauld.ac.uk/learn/family-activities/if-buildings-could-talk

This learning resource has a number of creative writing activities using photographs from the Courtauld Institute's Conway Library, which has an archive of over 1 million photographs of architecture from around the world spanning all periods to the present day.

Creative writing: The Mayflower

www.museumsworcestershire.org.uk/collections/activities

Create a piece of writing based on one of the Mayflower Pilgrims. Select from Activities based on the Curriculum.

Grace Darling: literacy skills

www.rnli.org/youth-education/education-resources/upper-primary/literacy-skills-lesson

A downloadable lesson plan to explore the life of Grace Darling by writing a diary from her perspective. Suitable for KS2.

How to make story sticks

www.scottishbooktrust.com/learning-resources/how-to-make-story-sticks

This activity can be used in the classroom or at home to generate creative ideas. Suitable for 6 to 16 years.

Japanese prints: creative writing

www.museumsworcestershire.org.uk/collections/activities

This has a writing prompts worksheet to help children write a story using pictures of 19th century Japanese woodblock prints for inspiration.

Just write

www.canalrivertrust.org.uk/explorers/resources

A literacy resource that encourages children to discover the waterways through writing their own poem or short story. Select Activities in the Filter by Subject/Topic.

Let's make a story: creative writing activity

www.salisburymuseum.org.uk/learning/family-learning

This is a downloadable worksheet to create a story. It has been designed by Salisbury Museum for children to write a story about objects found in the Medieval drains of Salisbury. This is a well-designed story writing template and would adapt well for other story writing ideas. If you like the idea of using unusual items to stimulate thinking, click the link on 'example objects' next to the worksheet resource link. Select Drainage Collection Story Activity from Resources for Families at Home.

Letter writing: pop it in the post

www.postalmuseum.org/visit-us/schools/learning-resources

Select Pop it in the Post for a learning resource designed by the Postal Museum aimed at KS1 and KS2 to discover the impact the Penny Black stamp had on our communication. It uses archive documents including photographs, stamps and letters to investigate the world's first prepaid postage stamp. A great resource to use as part of literacy or creative writing in the classroom or at home.

Letter writing: World War 2 – life as an evacuee

www.cimuseums.org.uk/museumfromhome

Write a letter home of your experience of being evacuated to a new area. Select Life as an Evacuee.

Letter writing: write home

www.britishlegion.org.uk/get-involved/remembrance/teaching-remembrance/ks2-lesson-plans

This resource from the Royal British Legion is a downloadable powerpoint and activity for children to consider the experience of those who left home to go to World War 2 and to write a postcard home about their experience. A very thoughtful and structured resource. Select Write Home in the Remembrance Bitesize section.

National Gallery: using paintings to inspire English or Drama

www.nationalgallery.org.uk/learning/teachers-and-schools/teaching-english-and-drama/how-to-read-a-painting

This is an extremely useful set of instructions and information on using paintings to structure ideas and discussion. The suggestions for developing ways of looking is particularly useful.

Oxford University Press: creative writing

https://global.oup.com/education/children/free-resources/creative-writing/?region=uk

A great resource for creative writing with downloadable activity sheets.

Pen Museum: activity sheets

www.penmuseum.org.uk/activity-sheets

Three interesting worksheets with ideas for creative writing.

Persuasive writing

https://education.cats.org.uk/teachers/lesson-plans

Select 7-9 English or 9-11 English for a thoughtful lesson plan for persuasive writing from the Cats Protection.

Persuasive writing: let's cycle more

www.bikeability.org.uk/tools-for-schools/learning-resources

Select KS2 Cycling and the Environment. This is a learning resource using persuasive writing to increase the number of people cycling, supporting their health and the environment. Excellent.

Report and journalistic writing

www.culturestreet.org.uk/teachers/shipwrecks/lessonplan.pdf
Inspired by a painting of a shipwreck, create a piece of writing in the style of a local newspaper for a defined audience.

Script writing: the characters of Lewis Carroll

www.culturestreet.org/lessons.php
Select The Characters of Lewis Carroll for a lesson plan for KS2 English script writing or developing writing for an audience.

Strength of character

www.schoolscience.co.uk/strengthofcharacter
An English-focused activity about the importance of characters in storytelling with a downloadable resource.

Windrush Stories: teaching resource for primary

www.bl.uk/teaching-resources/windrush-stories-primary-creative-writing
Teaching resources from the British Library for primary creative writing and activities using histories, people and objects featured on the Windrush Stories Online resource. The use of archives, images, documents and articles is excellent.

Writing skills for secondary

Creative writing: Victorian film in the classroom

www2.bfi.org.uk/education-research/education/teaching-victorian-film
These are highly original lesson ideas and resources for English Literature and Language KS3 and KS4 inspired by Victorian film. The Vibrant Victorians includes a collection of creative writing tasks inspired by ten early silent films from the British Film Institute.

News literacy resource toolkit (Economist Educational Foundation)

www.economistfoundation.org/news-literacy
The news literacy model has been created by the Economist Educational Foundation as a way to support the development of news literacy in young people. It outlines the knowledge and skills needed to engage with the news. The model includes a News Curriculum, which details the specific knowledge required to understand the news. It also sets out four essential critical thinking and communication skills: speaking, listening, problem-solving and creativity. These skills form part of the Skills Builder Universal Framework (**www.skillsbuilder.org**).

The resources are for teachers to help with use of the news literacy model in the classroom and are suitable for children and young people from 9 to 16 years. Excellent.

Persuasive creative writing

www.amnesty.org.uk/resources/lessons-writing-impossible-circumstances

Two downloadable lessons produced by Amnesty International and the Anne Frank Trust to explore Anne Frank's life and legacy through the context of the right to freedom of expression and opinion. It includes a powerpoint, resource sheets with teacher notes and an activity to undertake a piece of persuasive creative writing.

A picture speaks a thousand words: exploring art, expanding literacy

www.yorkmuseumstrust.org.uk/education/schools-2-2/york-art-gallery-downloads

York City Gallery has produced a resource pack for secondary pupils. The activity asks the child to focus on one work of art and uses it to inspire them to write creatively through a series of games and activities. This can be done with any image or picture within the classroom or at home. It is based on a project inspired by Ron Mueck's sculpture 'Youth' (2009).

Windrush stories: teaching resource for secondary

www.bl.uk/teaching-resources/windrush-stories-secondary-creative-writing

Teaching resources form the British Library for secondary creative writing and activities using histories, people and objects featured on the Windrush Stories Online resource. The use of archives, images, documents and articles is excellent

FAMOUS AND INSPIRATIONAL PEOPLE

Knowing who's who and what they did and why is not only fascinating but illuminating too. The significance of fame can be more than we think, as we relate the person to historical events that changed or shaped our world, to discoveries that had impact on our lives or movements that influenced our culture. There are lots of learning resources below for a variety of famous names.

You might also like to try the *Guinness World Records Hall of Fame* **www.guinnessworldrecords.com/records/hall-of-fame**, which is fascinating and includes more than just the world's tallest man!

Information

40 inspirational children

www.goodhousekeeping.com/life/inspirational-stories/g5188/kids-who-changed-the-world

A good starting point for finding out about contemporary children activists along with some inspirational children from the past.

Famous people

www.teachingideas.co.uk

Select Themes, then Famous People, for a host of cross-curricular teaching ideas and resources. This has lots of activities, lesson plans and resources to download. It is fantastic for teachers and parents with children learning at home. It includes printable banners for displays, which would be useful for classrooms, libraries and home use.

Famous people: biographies

www.ducksters.com/biography

This is a good starting point for identifying the main players for a period of history or for a list of World Leaders; Women Leaders; Civil Rights Heroes; Inventors and Scientists; Entrepreneurs; Artists; and Explorers. The information given for each named person is certainly well structured and the list of famous people is quite extensive. However, there is a concentration on historical figures and a lack of contemporary figures included.

Famous Scots

www.visitscotland.com/about/famous-scots

This provides a list of famous Scottish people with information and places related to the individual.

Interviews with famous children's authors and artists

www.bl.uk/childrens-books/themes/interviews

A fascinating and very useful set of interviews with children's authors and illustrators, including: Jacqueline Wilson; Zanib Mian; Julia Donaldson; Joseph Coelho; Michael Rosen; SF Said; Andy Stanton; Quentin Blake; Axel Scheffler; and Viviane Schwartz. Find out how they got started and their earliest inspiration.

National Geographic Kids: famous people

www.natgeokids.com/uk/teacher-category/significant-people

Primary resources to download for a host of well-known significant and historical people. Well worth looking at.

Women of science

www.nls.uk/learning-zone/science-and-technology

Learn about pioneering Scottish women of science.

Famous individuals

Ada Lovelace

www.natgeokids.com/uk/primary-resource/ada-lovelace-primary-resource

Find out about mathematician Ada Lovelace and her role in computer programming.

Andrew Carnegie

www.carnegiebirthplace.com/history-resources

Find out about Andrew Carnegie, once the richest man in the world, philanthropist and founder of the free Carnegie Libraries in the US and UK.

Anne Boleyn

www.hrp.org.uk/schools/learning-resources

The Story of Anne Boleyn video resource from the Historic Royal Palaces. Suitable for KS2 and KS3. Select Tudors from the Topic list.

Anne Frank

www.natgeokids.com/uk/primary-resource/anne-frank-primary-resource

A resource sheet that helps pupils learn about the life of Anne Frank and how her famous diary has become an important part of world history.

Anne Frank: writing in impossible circumstances

www.amnesty.org.uk/resources/lessons-writing-impossible-circumstances

There are two downloadable lessons produced by Amnesty International and the Anne Frank Trust to explore Anne Frank's life and legacy through the context of the right to freedom of expression and opinion. It includes a powerpoint, resource sheets and learning and teacher notes. Excellent.

Charles Dickens

www.bl.uk/people/charles-dickens

Explore the life and work of Charles Dickens with this British Library resource, which also links to related teaching resources.

Ernest Shackleton

www.nls.uk/learning-zone/geography-and-exploration/shackleton-and-wordie

Find out about explorer Ernest Shackleton, the Imperial Trans-Antarctic Expedition of 1914-1917 and the expedition's Scottish geologist, James Wordie.

Gertrude Bell: the great adventurer

www.dormanmuseum.co.uk

Find out about Gertrude Bell the adventurer, travel-writer and World War 1 spy. Select Local Hero: Gertrude Bell Activity Pack.

Grace Darling

www.rnli.org/youth-education/education-resources/lower-primary/topic-pack

A downloadable pack containing six lesson plans themed around the life of Grace Darling. For children aged 3-7.

Florence Nightingale

www.museumcrush.org/life-beyond-the-lady-of-the-lamp-the-photograph-of-86-year-old-florence-nightingale

This gives an insight into Florence Nightingale's later years and the impact she had on transforming healthcare and nursing and depicts a number of artefacts.

Francis Drake

www.rmg.co.uk/discover/teacher-resources/starter-ideas-life-and-times-francis-drake

The life and times of Francis Drake as a lesson plan for teachers.

Guy Fawkes

www.hrp.org.uk

The story of Guy Fawkes and the Gunpowder Plot. Select History & Stories and then Stuart. Excellent.

Henry VIII

www.hrp.org.uk

Select History and Stories, then Henry VIII.

Henry Moore

www.henry-moore.org/about-henry-moore/biography

Find out about the sculptor Henry Moore's life. Includes a timeline.

James Watt

www.birminghammuseums.org.uk/school_resources/local-people-james-watt

Facts and activities to learn about Scottish engineer, chemist and inventor James Watt.

Lady Jane Grey

www.hrp.org.uk

The story of Lady Jane Grey. Select Schools, Learning Resources, then Tudors from the Topic list.

Leonardo Da Vinci

www.natgeokids.com/uk/primary-resource/leonardo-da-vinci-primary-resource

This primary teaching resource introduces children to painter and inventor Leonardo da Vinci.

Martin Luther King Jr

www.natgeokids.com/uk/primary-resource/martin-luther-king-jr-primary-resource

Find out about Martin Luther King Jr and his role in the Civil Rights Movement.

Mary Anning

www.geolsoc.org.uk/factsheets#Mary%20Anning

www.lymeregismuseum.co.uk/collection/mary-anning

Find out about the story of Mary Anning the fossil hunter.

Mary Queen of Scots

www.historicenvironment.scot/learn/learning-resources/teaching-resources/#themed-resources_tab

Select Mary Queen of Scots from the Themed Resources for a downloadable resource of the life of Mary and a timeline of events.

Mary Seacole

www.npg.org.uk/learning/digital/history/mary-seacole

Short learning resource using a rare portrait of Mary Seacole to stimulate discussion and investigation into her life.

Mary Shelley

www.bl.uk/people/mary-shelley

Explore the life and work of Mary Shelley with this British Library resource, which also links to related online resources.

Michael Faraday

www.rigb.org/our-history/michael-faraday

Find out about the scientist Michael Faraday from the Royal Institution.

Michael Morpurgo

www.michaelmorpurgo.com

Find out about children's author Michael Morpurgo.

Neil Armstrong

www.natgeokids.com/uk/primary-resource/neil-armstrong-primary-resource

Discover Neil Armstrong and how he became the first man on the Moon.

Nelson Mandela

www.natgeokids.com/uk/primary-resource/nelson-mandela-primary-resource

Introduces one of the world's most famous human rights activists, Nelson Mandela, and how he dedicated his life to the struggle against racism and discrimination.

Pablo Picasso

www.natgeokids.com/uk/primary-resource/pablo-picasso-art-primary-resource

Learn about artist Pablo Picasso's life and works and the influence they have had on modern day artistic styles.

Roald Dahl

www.natgeokids.com/uk/primary-resource/roald-dahl-english-primary-resource
www.roalddahl.com.roald-dahl/about

All about Roald Dahl, including a timeline and The Roald Dahl archive.

Robert the Bruce

www.culturenl.co.uk/museums/learning-museums

Find out about Robert the Bruce. Select Learning at Home, then Museum at Home, then Knights and Castles.

Robert Louis Stevenson

www.bl.uk/people/robert-louis-stevenson

Explore the life and work of Robert Louis Stevenson with this British Library resource, which also links to related online resources.

Rosa Parks

www.natgeokids.com/uk/primary-resource/rosa-parks-primary-resource

Find out about civil rights campaigner Rosa Parks.

St George and the Dragon

www.hartleburycastle.com/activities/#informationsheets

Information sheet to learn about St George and the Dragon.

William Shakespeare

www.rsc.org.uk/shakespeares-life-and-times

Shakespeare's life and times from the Royal Shakespeare Company.

HOME-SCHOOL LEARNING RESOURCES

www.shakespearesglobe.com/discover/shakespeares-world/william-shakespeare
Find out about William Shakespeare with the Globe Theatre.

www.natgeokids.com/uk/primary-resource/shakespeare-primary-resource
Discover interesting facts about William Shakespeare.

FILM AND PHOTOGRAPHY

The use of archive film or photographs can certainly bring topics and subjects to life, especially History, Citizenship, English and Art. For a royalty-free photographic archive try UK Photo and Social History Archive (**www.ukphotoarchive.org.uk**). For more current film information, children and young people may be interested in BAFTA Kids (**www.baftakids.org**), the Bafta Organisation's platform for 7 - 14-year- olds to discover films and television. In addition, to find locations where some of the UK's most iconic films and TV shows have been filmed visit **www.visitbritain.com/gb/en/things-to-do/film-and-tv#.**

Film

Learning resources and activities

British Council Film Archive

https://film.britishcouncil.org./resources/film-archive

Over 100 short documentaries about wartime Britain made by the British Council during the 1940s.

British Film Institute: learning resources

www2.bfi.org.uk/education-research/teaching-film-tv-media-studies

This has teaching and learning materials for teaching with, or about, film. It has film resources for Sci-Fi in the classroom; Gothic in the classroom and Black Star education. For each, there are films to watch and resources to use to explore the film, linking to curriculum subjects. These are excellent resources with great originality to use at home or in the classroom.

Moving Image Archive

https://movingimage.nls.uk

This is a fantastic resource to explore with around 100 years of Scotland's history from both amateur and professional film makers. There are 1000s of films from the National Library of Scotland archives. It has a simple search facility that makes this brilliant resource even more attractive. Excellent.

Screen Online

www.screenonline.org.uk

Select Education for access to films and television titles from 1890 to 2014. Access the Lesson Bank for links to curriculum subjects covering English, History, Geography, Citizenship, Science, Music, Art and Design, MFL and RE, not to mention Film and Media Studies and the Performing Arts. This has some amazing films and documentaries with detailed lesson plans. Fantastic to use in the classroom or for learning at home. Excellent.

Photography

Belfast Exposed: photographs archive

www.belfastexposed.org

With over 1 million photographs that record the political, cultural and social change in Northern Ireland, including The Troubles, this is an important resource for photography students.

Make your own pinhole camera

www.theboxplymouth.com/schools/learning-resources/make-your-own-pinhole-camera

Suitable for KS2.

Make a pinhole camera

www.scarboroughmuseumstrust.com/art-gallery-resources

Select Pinhole Camera for a short downloadable resource on how to make a pinhole camera. Inspired by pictures of the seaside.

World War 1: War Photographer – Ernest Brooks

www.britishlegion.org.uk/get-involved/remembrance/teaching-remembrance/ks4-lesson-plans

This is a resource for KS4 developed by the Royal British Legion to investigate remembrance and the role of war photography to record the impact of war. Excellent for students looking at the art of photography and its role in journalism and communication.

FLAGS

When looking at countries and identity, flags are an important source of information and of historical significance.

Information

Flag Detective

www.flagdetective.com

This is an easy-to-use flag identification tool, identifying flags by country as well as world organisations. It also enables finding flags by type, allowing us all to know the difference between a Canton and Saltire flag, along with the sixteen other flag types. Excellent.

World flags database

www.flags.net

Includes national flags, ensigns, military flags and head-of-state flags, with beautiful illustrations. For teachers, parents and students.

Learning Resources and Activities

Flags of the World

www.fotw.info

Packed with information and images of flags of countries, organisations, territories, districts and cities, both past and present. It has useful printable flag images located under Colouring Book (these are templates of flags for colouring).

C GEOGRAPHY

See also: Citizenship; Population

Geography is both a vast and fascinating subject. It encompasses physical, human and environmental topics, not to mention geology, map-reading, weather and climate change. Its impact on our lives is more than most of us can imagine and for this reason it is an important subject for children and young people to investigate. Fortunately, there are a number of excellent organisations, such as the Royal Geographic Society, that provide information and learning resources to support the study and understanding of geography and related issues. The resources below are arranged to include organisations offering a package of geography topics followed by those focusing on specific aspects. These include: the Environment; Natural Disasters; Tourism; Water; and Weather (Climate Change). Resources for Geology are also provided.

Learning resources and activities

Primary school teaching ideas

www.teachingideas.co.uk

Select Other Subjects, then Geography. This has downloadable teaching resources, ideas and activities. It includes fieldwork, local area geography, rivers, natural disasters and much more. Excellent.

The Geography Site

www.geography-site.co.uk

An amazing site covering all aspects of geography: human, physical and environmental. It is useful for primary and secondary children for information and definitions on many topics covered in KS2 and KS3. Well worth a visit.

The Geological Society

www.geolsoc.org.uk

This is packed with resources. Select Education and Careers, then Teaching Resources and Activities. This includes a set of factsheets from volcanoes to earthquakes and from minerals to energy. There is a section providing lesson plans and links to Earth Science classroom activities that could be used at home as well. Excellent.

National Geographic Kids: primary geography resources

www.natgeokids.com/uk/teacher-category/geography

This provides teaching resources that support the geography curriculum for both the National Curriculum and the Scottish Curriculum for Excellence. In addition, it has plenty of KS1 and KS2 teaching and learning ideas and fun facts for Early Years. Excellent.

Royal Geographic Society

www.rgs.org/schools/teaching-resources

Absolutely brilliant and packed with high-quality geographical teaching and learning resources for a wealth of topics for all key stages. Includes COVID-19; Food and Food Crisis; Extreme Weather; Natural Disasters; Population; Migration; Urbanisation; and many more. Excellent.

Royal Mint: learning resources

www.royalmint.com/kids

Select Geography Pack for a downloadable resource called *Coins in the Classroom* looking at coins from around the world.

Maps and map-reading

British Library teaching resources: geography

www.bl.uk/teaching-resources?curriculum=uk

Select Geography from the Subject list. This includes downloadable teaching resources from the British Library on map-making and map-reading skills for ages 7-11, 14-16 and 16-18.

Get your bearings: maps

www.chatsworth.org/your-visit/learning/learning-resources/resources-for-ages-5-7

This is a learning resource to explore maps at home. Suitable for KS1 and KS2. Select Get Your Bearings: Maps (geography).

Get your bearings: compasses

www.chatsworth.org/your-visit/learning/learning-resources/resources-for-ages-5-7

Explore using a compass and learn the order of the four and the eight compass points. Suitable for KS1 and KS2. Select Get Your Bearings: Compasses (geography).

Prisoners of Geography Our World Explained in 12 Simple Maps: teachers notes

www.simonandschuster.co.uk/c/Activity-Sheets

This has a great set of teachers notes to use with the book *Prisoners of Geography*, which gives an overview of the world. It explores each country and its geography, looking at climate, physical geography and natural resources. Select Non-Fiction - Prisoners of Geography.

You are here: 10 things you need to know about maps

www.nls.uk/learning-zone/geography-and-exploration

An exploration of maps and what they are from the National Library of Scotland. It features interactive quizzes and downloadable learning activities. Select You Are Here.

World atlas

www.worldatlas.com

This provides maps for all continents and countries of the world. Within the Continent facility you can click for a full picture of all the countries within the specific continent, then click on a specific country for a map, brief country history, flag and quick facts relating to land area, population and currency. Also includes links to a country's symbols and details of their flag and national anthem. Furthermore, within the World facility there are environment articles that cover different topics and are packed with facts and commentary. There are also World Facts, again presented as articles with colour photographs. Well worth exploring.

Topics

Environment

Cycling in my local community

www.bikeability.org.uk/tools-for-schools/learning-resources

Select KS1 Geography then Cycling in My Local Community for learning resources on researching the local community and investigating opportunities to cycle and plan routes.

Environment: teaching ideas

www.teachingideas.co.uk/themes/the-environment

This has teaching and learning materials linked to the environment for KS1 and KS2. It includes teaching resources, activities and ideas that can be used in the classroom or at home. Excellent.

Environmental change: film resources

www.greatnorthmuseum.org.uk/learning/film-resources

A series of films from the Great North Museum on aspects of environmental change.

Museum of Zoology: our changing planet

www.museumofzoologyblog.com/category/nature-classroom

Explore our evolving planet with resources linked to current research. Suitable for KS3 and KS4 and considers climate change and changing landscapes. Select Our Changing Planet.

Sustainability in packaging: learning resource

www.museumofbrands.com/online-resources

This learning resource from the Museum of Brands explores packaging and how we can try to stop the packaging we use from damaging the Earth. There are two downloads: one for KS2 and one for KS3 and GCSE. Excellent.

The vivarium: it all starts with you

www.mmfromhome.com/resource-for-home-educators-and-fam

Manchester Museum has produced an extensive set of simple environmental worksheets for KS1 and KS2 looking at Rainforests. They include lots of useful activities that could be done at home or in the classroom. Scroll down and select The Vivarium.

Young People's Trust for the Environment

www.ypte.org.uk

This has hundreds of resources to help teach children about the environment and the need to develop and live sustainably. It includes an incredible set of A-Z factsheets on animals and the environment, from Aardvark to Zoos. It has Home Learning Packs to support parents and carers and their children. For teenagers it has articles and videos on the environment. For teachers and educators there are lesson plans covering the African Savanna; Climate Change; Evolution; Food Miles; Plastic Pollution; Rainforests; and the Water Cycle, along with many more. In addition, it has a collection of useful downloads from Conservation Education. Well worth looking at. Excellent.

Geology

Big Jurassic classroom resources

www.jurassiccoast.org/what-is-the-jurassic-coast/things-to-do/jurassic-coast-teachers-resources

A downloadable resource to support the teaching of rocks, fossils and evolution developed by the Primary Science Teaching Trust in conjunction with the Jurassic Coast Trust. It has a downloadable book that brings together resources and information to show teachers and educators how they can use their local environments to inspire interest in the UK's geological history. The activity pack provides images, worksheets and activity instructions for children aged 3-7 and 7-11. In addition, there are further resources available to download on the theme of the Jurassic Coast and links to factsheets from the Geological Society. Excellent.

British Geological Society

www.bgs.ac.uk/discovering-geology

This introduces geoscience topics to schools and young people to help them discover geology and our changing planet. It includes rocks and minerals, climate change and geological processes. Excellent.

Dartmoor National Park: factsheets

www.dartmoor.gov.uk/learning/basic-factsheets

A series of factsheets, including one on the rocks of Dartmoor.

Dartmoor National Park: learning resources

www.dartmoor.gov.uk/learning/teachers-educators

This has downloadable resources for KS2 and KS3 on Mires, Peat and Bogs; Bronze Age Dartmoor; and exploring Biodiversity.

National Coal Mining Museum: coal

www.ncm.org.uk/learrning/learning-resources/science

Scroll down to Rock Factsheets for resources to find out how coal was formed and its properties.

National Coal Mining Museum: rocks and minerals

www.ncm.org.uk/learning/learning-resources/mining-factsheets

This has mining factsheets on Coal, Rocks and Minerals and Properties of Rocks.

Oxford University Museum of Natural History: learning zone

www.oum.ox.ac.uk/thezone

Designed for younger children to find facts and information on rocks and minerals.

Rock, fossils and energy

www.nationalminingmuseum.com/learning/learning-at-home-with-national-mining-museum-scotland

This learning resource from the National Mining Museum Scotland gives facts about coal and fossils with a great range of related activities. Look also at the film Fossil Fuel Formation Complete at: **www.nationalminingmuseum.com/fossil-fuel-formation-vimeo**

Salt in Cheshire

www.lionsaltworks.westcheshiremuseums.co.uk/whatissalt

This has a downloadable information sheet on salt in Cheshire and how it affects the local landscape.

Natural disasters

The Geological Society: earthquakes

www.geolsoc.org.uk/earthquakes

Includes factsheets, online interactive resources and information.

The Geological Society: flooding

www.geolsoc.org.uk/flooding

Resources include factsheets and podcasts.

The Geological Society: volcanoes

www.geolsoc.org.uk/volcanoes

Includes factsheets, online interactive resources and activities. Excellent.

Tourism

National Parks

www.nationalparks.uk/teaching-resources

National Parks UK has produced an excellent set of teaching resources that can be incorporated into the curriculum for England, Wales and Scotland, to complement learning on climate change, habitats and tourism, along with understanding the importance of national parks.

Water

Convection currents

www.museum.wales/cardiff/learning/resources

Investigate ocean currents and the effect temperature has on the movement of fluids with Cardiff Museum. This includes downloadable activity sheets. Select Convection Currents.

Dŵr Cymru Welsh Water

https://corporate.dwrcymru.com/community/education

This provides teaching resources for primary and secondary with activities linked to the curriculum on all aspects of water.

Unravelling rivers

www.canalrivertrust.org.uk/explorers/resources

This provides an introduction to how rivers are formed and flow from source to mouth. It is suitable for Y5 and Y6 but could be adapted for younger children. It includes activity sheets and a lesson plan for teachers. Select to filter by Environment and then select Unravelling Rivers. Excellent.

Water Aid

www.wateraid.org/uk/get-involved/all/schools-and-teachers

Packed with resources for school and home learning. Select either KS1, KS2, KS3 or KS4.

Water: facts

www.natgeokids.com/uk/primary-resource/water-facts-primary-resource

This has learning resources on water for KS1 and KS2.

Water KS2

www.wateraid.org.uk/uk/get-involved/teaching/ks2-resources

Lesson plans for looking at water and water issues. These can be used both in school and at home.

Water KS3 & KS4

www.wateraid.org/uk/get-involved/teaching/ks3-resources
www.wateraid.org/uk/get-involved/teaching/ks4-resources

Lessons plans to cover the water and sanitation crisis and explores human rights in relation to water.

Water Cycle

www.yorkshirewater.com/education

Select Learning to find out about the Water Cycle or access Home Learning for activities related to water. There are teacher resources available here too.

Water Cycle: experiment

www.discoverymuseum.org.uk/water

Explore the Water Cycle and make your own mini water cycle experiment.

Water Cycle: KS2 resources

www.wateraid.org/uk/get-involved/teaching/ks2-resources

Select the Water Cycle for a lesson plan on the stages of the water cycle.

Weather (including climate change)

Changing climates curriculum

www.thoughtboxeducation.com/climate-resources

This extensive resource from ThoughtBox offers lessons by age 5-7, 7-9, 9-11, 11-13, 13-15 and 15-18 about the cause and effect of climate change. It looks at the impact of climate change and how young people can be empowered to be global change-makers. ThoughtBox allows individuals to register to access the free resources, which is certainly worth doing and is ideal for parents. Excellent.

Climate Kids

www.climatekids.nasa.gov

Explore climate with NASA. This looks at some of the big topical questions such as What is Climate Change?; Why is Carbon important?; What is the Greenhouse Effect?; How do we know the Climate is Changing?; and more. It has sections on Weather and Climate; Atmosphere; Water; Energy; and Plants and Animals, all of which are beautifully produced into topics or issues, with information and colourful photographs and images to support.

Climate change: conservation in the classroom

www.worldwildlife.org/teaching-resources

Select Conservation in the Classroom. There is a film on climate change followed by a climate change worksheet.

Climate change: poster

www.derbymuseumsfromhome.com/activities/climate-change-poster

Find out and think about climate change then create a poster. This includes a video and downloadable activity sheet. Suitable for 7 years+.

Climate change: teaching ideas

www.greatnorthmuseum.org.uk/learning/museum-activities-from-home-or-school

This is a resource for teachers and educators for KS1 and KS2 for teaching ideas on climate change topics. Select Teaching Ideas for Climate Change.

Earth Heroes: teaching resources pack

www.nosycrow.com/resource/earth-heroes-teaching-resource-pack

Wonderful resource to support the use of the book *Earth Heroes* by Lily Dyu, exploring how campaigners like Greta Thunberg and David Attenborough are a beacon of hope in the fight for the future of our planet. Excellent.

Extreme weather

www.economistfoundation.org/resources/#climate-change

Select Extreme Weather for a six-session resource from the Economist Educational Foundation. It explores the impact of extreme weather and is packed with information, discussion and analysis with top quality production. Excellent.

Greta's Story: chapter by chapter resources by Valentina Camerini

www.simonandschuster.co.uk/c/Activity-Sheets

A resource to use with the book *Greta's Story* and to consider the issues raised by Greta Thunberg. Select *Greta's Story* in the Non-fiction section.

How to talk to children about the Climate Crisis

www.barnowltrust.org.uk

Select the Kids' Stuff tab. This is a brilliant resource from ThoughtBox Education. It explores climate change starting with a brief history (a must-read for us all) and then asks what we can do. It gives further resources to learn more. Suitable for families and schools. Excellent.

National Geographic Kids: weather

www.natgeokids.com/uk/teacher-category/weather

This provides weather resources for primary age children. It covers Climate Change, Extreme Weather, the Arctic and Antarctica.

Weather: The Meteorological Office

www.metoffice.gov.uk/weather/learn-about/met-office-for-schools

The Meteorological Office provides excellent learning resources linked to the curriculum covering five key themes: Forecasting and Predication; Extreme Weather;

Weather and Climate Stories; Technology and Innovation in Weather; and People in Weather and Climate. The resources are suitable for ages 7 to 11 and 11 to 14.

It also has bitesize hands-on activities to use in the classroom or to do at home, along with fun games and activities to discover more about the weather.

HEALTH AND WELLBEING

See also: Change and loss; Citizenship; Drugs, alcohol and smoking, PSHE (Personal, Health, Social and Economic Education); Relationships and sex

This topic has a lot of crossovers with other areas depending on what specific aspect of health and wellbeing is required. It is worth checking Citizenship, for example, if you are discussing online safety with your child or at school with a class or PSHE for further resources linked to mental health and wellbeing. Fortunately there are many fantastic organisations, dedicated to children and young people's health, who have created resources to use in school or at home.

Information

Family Lives: primary-age children

www.familylives.org.uk/advice/primary

This provides information for parents on supporting primary-age children with the issues that may affect their health and wellbeing.

Family Lives: secondary-age children

www.familylives.org.uk/advice/secondary/health-and-development

This provides information and advice to parents on talking with young people about issues that affect their health and wellbeing.

KidsHealth

www.kidshealth.org

This is a great site for children, young people and their parents, providing heaps of information on health issues and staying healthy. Although the site is American, the For Educators section is well worth using for material for lesson plans for teachers and for parents/carers to use at home. It includes downloadable worksheets, posters and teacher guides. Excellent.

World Cancer Research Fund: healthy living for kids

www.wcrf.org/eat-move-learn/about

The Eat-Move-Learn team teaches 7-11-year-olds about healthy eating and being active in a fun way. The concept has been developed by the World Cancer Research Fund. There are four cartoon characters: Mixer for healthy eating; Pedal for activity; Searcher for all the facts about fitness and food; and Flower the gardener. Each character has bitesize activities to do at home linked to teaching children how to stay healthy. Excellent.

You and your body

www.childline.org.uk/info-advice/you-your-body/#explore

Excellent coverage for drugs, alcohol and smoking, as well as puberty, staying healthy and living with disability. It also has a section dedicated to Coronavirus.

Young people and their health

www.healthtalk.org

Select Go to the A-Z, then Y on the HealthTalk topic listing. This has young people talking about a range of health issues via a series of interviews. All the topic areas covered are very informative and allow further discussion with young people either at home or within the classroom. It also provides further help and resources with links to other organisations. Excellent.

Specific health topics

COVID-19

COVID-19 booklist to support children and families

www.reading-well.org.uk/news/covid19children

This booklist has been created in partnership with ASCEL (Association of Senior Children's and Education Librarians), Libraries Connected and the Reading Agency to support children and families during the COVID-19 pandemic. Many of the books included are available from the publishers as free downloadable e-books and have been created specially to support children and young people during COVID-19. Excellent.

Mentally Healthy Schools: coronavirus

www.mentallyhealthyschools.org.uk/risks-and-protective-factors/coronavirus-supporting-childrens-mental-health

Guidance and practical tools to support children's mental health during the COVID-19 pandemic. This has excellent resources for children, schools and parents with links to further resources. Highly recommended.

NSPCC: COVID-19

www.nspcc.org.uk/keeping-children-safe/childrens-mental-health/depression-anxiety-mental-health

The NSPCC offers lots of advice on things to do to support children and young people worrying about COVID-19.

Partnership for Families: COVID-19

www.partnershipforchildren.org.uk/what-we-do/childrens-wellbeing-activities-for-teaching-staff-and-families.html

These are resources to help children find healthy ways to deal with their feelings and reactions to the COVID-19 pandemic. There are excellent downloadable resources for both teachers and families to use covering issues such as coping with the death of a loved one and life after lockdown. Some of the activities are available in other languages, including Bulgarian; Danish; Polish; Portuguese; French and Spanish.

Feelings and mental health

Childline: toolbox

www.childline.org.uk/toolbox

A host of games, videos and activities to help young people express their feelings and handle their emotions. Excellent.

Children's mental health

www.nspcc.org.uk/keeping-children-safe/childrens-mental-health

The NSPCC offers advice and information on how to talk to and support children with depression, anxiety and mental health, including dealing with self-harm.

Emotional wellbeing resources

www.downs-syndrome.org.uk/for-families-and-carers/emotional-well-being-resources

This offers a fantastic set of accessible resources to support the emotional wellbeing of children and adults with Down's Syndrome along with their parents, carers and families. It includes resources on feelings, anger, bullying, stress and relaxation. These would be great not only for home use but also within the classroom. Excellent.

Explore Bethlem: inside a nineteenth-century psychiatric hospital

www.museumofthemind.org.uk/learning

Bethlem Museum of the Mind has designed an interesting resource to encourage discussion about mental wellbeing for KS3. It includes a replica London Bethlem Hospital floorplan, which allows the user to visit each room for information, images, patient profiles and lesson plans in order to explore some of the issues around mental health and wellbeing. Excellent.

Loneliness and young people

www.redcross.org.uk/get-help/get-help-with-loneliness/tackling-loneliness-in-young-people

A fantastic set of mental health and wellbeing tools to reduce feelings of loneliness in young people. The information and activities have been developed by the British Red Cross in partnership with the Department of Digital, Culture, Media and Sport (DCMS).

The Maze by William Kurelak

www.museumofthemind.org.uk/learning/the-maze

Analysis of the painting 'The Maze' and the artist's own interpretation.

Time to Change: mental health resources for teachers

www.time-to-change.org.uk/get-involved/get-involved-schools/mental-health-resources-teachers

Time to Change provides downloadable resources and material to deliver a mental health assembly or to use within school for displays or group work, as well as when talking to parents.

The Usborne Mental Health and Wellbeing Resource Pack

www.usborne.com/gb/schools/teachers-resources-and-activities/all

This resource pack focuses upon recognising and understanding feelings and can be used with children from EYFS to KS2. Use a keyword search for *Usborne Mental Health and Wellbeing Resource Pack.*

Your feelings

www.childline.org.uk/info-advice/your-feelings/#explore

Excellent coverage for young people on feelings and emotions; anxiety; stress; panic; mental health; self-harm; eating problems; sexual and gender identity.

Healthy eating (and eating disorders)

Healthy eating for children: food factsheet

www.bda.uk.com/resource/healthy-eating-for-children.html

A food factsheet from the Association of UK Dietitians. It has extensive information and links to further information.

Mentally Healthy Schools: eating problems

www.mentallyhealthyschools.org.uk/mental-health-needs/eating-problems

Excellent information and resources dealing with eating difficulties.

NHS: food facts

www.nhs.uk/change4life/food-facts

This has learning modules covering Salt; Saturated Fat; Food Labels; Sugar; and Snacks. These are aimed at families to consider and think about healthy eating.

The RHS Big Soup Share

https://schoolgardening.rhs.org.uk/competitions/big-soup-share

The Big Soup Share is an annual event in October and the resources and recipes are available to download after the event. This is great for encouraging healthy eating in a fun way and can be used at school or at home.

Young Minds: eating problems

www.youngminds.org.uk/find-help/feelings-and-symptoms/eating-problems

Excellent information and resources from Young Minds dealing with eating difficulties.

Heart

British Heart Foundation: children and young people

www.bhf.org.uk/informationsupport/support/children-and-young-people

Information and resources for young people with a heart condition.

Staying safe

First aid

British Red Cross: first aid teaching resources

www.redcross.org.uk/get-involved/teaching-resources/first-aid-and-the-bystander-effect-teaching-resources

These resources are designed to give children and young people the skills, confidence and willingness to act when someone is in need of first aid. It covers the curriculum requirements for teaching first aid in primary and secondary schools in England. Excellent.

St John Ambulance: first aid

www.sja.org.uk/get-advice/key-stage-first-aid-lesson-plans

From September 2020, all state-funded schools in England are required to teach first aid as part of health education for all key stages. St John Ambulance has created downloadable first aid lesson plans and teaching resources for KS2, KS3 and KS4. The content is excellent and has been designed for use at school or for home learning. Furthermore, these resources are not just about cuts and bruises but seriously tackle empowering young people to be aware of dealing with a range of emergencies they may encounter at home or at school, such as asthma and choking and many more. Excellent.

Online Safety

Childline: e-safety

www.childline.org.uk/info-advice/bullying-abuse-safety/online-mobile-safety/staying-safe-online

This has fantastic advice and information on how to stay safe and how to be aware of the dangers of going online and using a mobile phone.

Childnet International: learning and teaching resources

www.childnet.com/young-people/primary

www.childnet.com/young-people/secondary

This has fantastic resources for young people, teachers, educators and parents/carers on keeping children safe online. There are a prolific number of resources including a PSHE toolkit for 11-14-year-olds. Excellent.

Digital resilience

www.drwg.org.uk

This has information on the digital resilience framework and resources pulled together by the Digital Resilience Working Group from the UKCIS (UK Council for Internet Safety). It is a must for teachers, educators and parents, bringing together a wealth of resources. Excellent.

Education for a connected world

www.gov.uk/government/publications/education-for-a-connected-world

This is a document from the UK Council for Internet Safety providing a framework to equip children and young people for digital life. It describes the digital knowledge and skills that children and young people should have.

Get Safe Online

www.getsafeonline.org/safeguarding-children

This has fantastic resources and information on keeping children and young people safe online. Topics include Clickjacking; Gaming; Cyberbullying; Cyberstalking; Texting and Sexting; and many more. It also includes checklists for parents to use by age group. Select under 5s, 6–9 years, 10–12 years or 13 years and over. Excellent.

Keep safe online

https://hwb.gov.wales/zones/keeping-safe-online

This has excellent resources from the Welsh government for children, young people, parents and teachers to use for online awareness and for guiding use. It is packed with well-presented and designed information including lesson plans. Excellent.

NSPCC: online safety

https://learning.nspcc.org.uk/safeguarding-child-protection-schools

Select Teaching Resources and then Online Safety for resources and lesson plans for keeping children safe online, e-safety for schools and Net Aware - looking at social media awareness. Excellent.

Online safety: anti-bullying from The Diana Award

www.antibullyingpro.com/resources

The Diana Award Anti-Bullying Campaign engages young people, parents and teachers to change the attitudes, behaviour and culture of bullying by building the skills and confidence to address different situations both online and offline. The resources are fantastic, beautifully produced and simply require a request for the download. Select Online Safety or Digital Wellbeing from the list of topics for a range of resources from videos, guides, activities, presentations and lesson plans. Fantastic for either classroom or home use.

Think U Know

www.thinkuknow.co.uk

Think U Know is an education programme from the National Crime Agency's Child Exploitation Online Protection (CEOP) Command. It provides educational resources including films, cartoons and lesson plans to help raise young people's awareness. It aims to ensure that everyone has access to information to keep children safe online. This includes children, young people, their parents and carers and the professionals who work with them. This is an excellent site, divided by age groups, which enables the information to be sensitively age appropriate. The Parent and Carer area is invaluable, with an online safety home activity pack to download that includes activities you can do at home with your children to support online safety. In addition, the Resource Library for professionals working with children and young people is packed with information, guidance, documents and toolkits to use with children. Excellent and recommended as priority reading for any parent/carer or teacher.

Travel safety

The Good Egg Guide to Cycling for Families

www.goodeggfamilycycling.com

A guide to cycling safely for all the family.

Road Safety Club: families and carers

www.tfl.gov.uk/info-for/schools-and-young-people/teaching-resources/road-safety-club

Offers downloadable activity sheets on road safety to use at home from Transport for London (TfL).

Road Safety: teaching resources for children

www.think.gov.uk/education-resources

Brilliant learning resources from the Think! campaign run by the Department for Transport, divided into age groups: 3-6, 7-12 and 13-16. It includes lesson plans, documents, slides and films. Excellent.

Travel safety

www.tfl.gov.uk/info-for/schools-and-young-people/safety-and-citizenship/lesson-plans

Fantastic set of resources to explore young people travelling independently. Many of the activities are related to any journey a child or young person may take not only using London tubes but walking, cycling and using the bus. There are extensive resources and lesson plans. Excellent resources for London schools and parents.

Walk about, talk about

www.tfl.gov.uk/info-for/schools-and-young-people/teaching-resources/walk-about-talk-about

This resource from Transport for London (TfL) looks at road safety and is aimed at pre-school children in London. It has five activities to do that cover crossing the road, safe places to cross and travelling safely. All the activity sheets are generic and would be great for use by Early Years and KS1 teachers and parents/carers and could easily be adapted for KS2. Excellent.

Water safety

Water safety

www.canalrivertrust.org.uk/explorers/resources

This provides an excellent set of downloadable resources, from posters to activity packs, designed for classroom and home use. Select Water Safety from the right-hand menu bar. Excellent.

Water safety from home

www.rnli.org/youth-education/water-safety-from-home

A downloadable learning and teaching resource from the Royal National Lifeboat Institution (RNLI) to educate children on water safety, including beach safety. There are primary and secondary teaching packs and video resources suitable for class or home use. Excellent.

Water safety resource

www.swimming.org/schools/resource-pack

A well-structured and comprehensive guide from Swim England on how children can keep safe around water. Excellent to use as a family or at school to alert young people to the dangers of water and how to enjoy water and swimming safely.

C HISTORY

See also: Citizenship; Famous and inspirational people; Inventions and discoveries; Olympics

With such a huge subject field it is hoped that the resources below offer some path through the mountain of materials and information available. There are many excellent organisations offering a wealth of learning resources covering more than one period of history or topic, such as the British Museum, the British Library or the Historical Association, and many more offering resources for a specific time or aspect of history, such the Children's University or the Jorvik Viking Centre. All levels are covered here from KS1 to KS4. The topics include: Ancient Civilisations; Anglo-Saxons; Vikings; Victorians; the Titanic; Black History; Suffrage; World War 1; and World War 2, plus many more in the alphabetical list below. In addition, there are some resources for Archaeology, Local History and Family History.

Learning resources and activities

Ashmolean Museum, Oxford: learning resources

www.ashmolean.org/learning-resources

Excellent downloadable learning resources including images and short films. Topics include Ancient Egypt; Ancient Greece; Ancient Rome; Ancient China; Prehistoric Britain; Anglo-Saxons; and Civil War England.

British Library: teaching resources – history

www.bl.uk/teaching-resources?curriculum=uk

Select History from the subject options. A huge amount of teaching resources for ages 5-7, 7-11, 11-14, 14-16 and 16-18, covering a wealth of themes that includes: Toys and Games; World War 1 and World War 2; Victorian Britain; Health and Hygiene; Colonisation; Propaganda; Georgian Britain; Medieval Living; Magna Carta; The Black Death; The Slave Trade; and many more. Each teaching resource is linked to related online resources. The material included is fantastic and offers a wealth of interest and ideas on the topics. Excellent.

British Museum

www.britishmuseum.org/learn/schools

The British Museum has a wealth of resources available to download covering a host of history topics. They are grouped by key stage - EYFS/KS1 (3-6); KS2(7-11); KS3 (11-14); KS4 (14-16); and KS5 (16+). The topics include: Ancient Britain; Ancient Egypt; Ancient Greece; Ancient Rome; Africa; Americas; Middle East; and Asia.

English Heritage: GCSE resources

www.english-heritage.org.uk/learn/teaching-resources/resource-library

English Heritage has a range of resources to support the study of the historic environment. The resources are organised by exam board schemes of work. Select Key Stage 4+ from Browse by Key Stage. Excellent.

English Heritage: teaching resources

www.english-heritage.org.uk/learn/teaching-resources

Excellent and vast amount of teaching resources from English Heritage developed by teachers, historians and experts to bring history to life in the classroom or at home. Topics include: Prehistory (Stone, Bronze and Iron Age); Romans; Anglo-Saxons and Normans; Medieval; Tudors and Stuarts; Victorians; and the 20th century. The teaching resources include downloadable activities and videos and are designed for work with KS1, KS2 and KS3.

Explore the past

https://research.ncl.ac.uk/explorethepastwithus/primaryschools
https://research.ncl.ac.uk/explorethepastwithus/secondaryschools

These are teaching and learning resources that have been developed by Newcastle University and the Great North Museum, Newcastle. They cover the Stone Age; Iron Age; Ancient Greece; Ancient Rome; and the Victorians.

Historic Royal Palaces: learning resources

www.hrp.org.uk

Select Schools, then Learning Resources. This has over 85 learning resources covering all key stages, SEND and home educators. The topics included are: Tudors; Victorians; Georgians; Medieval; Elizabethans; Stuarts; Normans; 20th and 21st century; Castles; Crime and Punishment; Wars; and the Historic Environment. The majority of resources are for classroom or home use with a few linked to visits to either the Tower of London; Hampton Court Palace; Kensington Palace; Banqueting House; or Hillsborough Castle. Excellent.

Historical Association: free resources

www.history.org.uk

The Historical Association has 1000s of free resources covering all periods and topics of history for each key stage. Use the search facility with the term 'free resources'. It is possible to filter by primary, secondary or student and to further refine within those groups. It also has resources for teachers. Excellent. Highly recommended.

History for kids

www.bbc.co.uk/history/forkids

Although this website is now archived and no longer updated, it is still excellent for a huge number of topics. It includes Ancient History, World History and British History.

History Learning Site

www.historylearningsite.co.uk

This covers a wealth of history topics for secondary and GCSE history. It includes: Ancient Rome; Medieval England; Nazi Germany; Tudor England; World War 1; and World War 2, along with many others. The amount of information available within each topic is extensive. Excellent.

Intriguing History

www.intriguing-history.com

This covers British History from the Roman period to the present day, using articles, posts, timelines, maps and artefacts, as well as looking at the people and personalities of the period. It looks at connections and context with the aim to see historic periods through fresh eyes. An extensive and indeed intriguing resource.

Maidstone Museum: learning resources

https://museum.maidstone.gov.uk/learn/learning-with-spike-at-home

This has an impressive set of downloadable School History Themes information and activity resources covering: Egyptians; Romans; Anglo-Saxons; Ancient Greeks; Dinosaurs (KS1); Mayans; and Toys (KS1).

Museum Crush

www.museumcrush.org/category/history

Museum Crush offers a wealth of history quick reads on curious finds and collections, discussing the significance and importance of what can be learnt about a historical event or a past way of life through investigating the artefacts. Absolutely fascinating and would enhance many history topics.

Museum of London: learning resources

www.museumoflondon.org.uk/schools/learning-resources

This has a range of history topics with resources linked to the Museum of London or the City of London. There are some films for topics that are very useful. Select by Foundation & Primary or Secondary to retrieve relevant topics.

National Archives

www.nationalarchives.gov.uk/education

Absolutely wonderful resources from the National Archives covering the following time periods: Medieval 974-1485; Early Modern 1485-1750; Empire and Industry 1750-1850; Victorians 1850-1901; Early 20th Century 1901-1918; Interwar 1918-1939; World War 2 1939-1945; and Post War 1945-present. For each time period, there are a wealth of topics and for each topic a host of information and worksheets based around archive material. It includes downloadable lesson packs, which are excellent not only for teachers but for home learning too.

National Geographic Kids: history primary resources

www.natgeokids.com/uk/teacher-category/history

This provides teaching resources to support the history curriculum as well as KS1 and KS2 teaching and learning ideas. It covers: Romans; Ancient Greeks; Anglo-Saxons; Ancient Egyptians and Vikings.

National Library of Wales: learning resources

www.library.wales/services/education/learning-resources

The National Library of Wales Education Service has produced a large number of outstanding learning resources for teachers in Wales, covering history topics that are covered in schools in Wales. The topics covered include the Industrial Revolution; World War 1; World War 2; and Warfare to Welfare 1939–1959. The level and quantity of material and information incorporated into the resources is commendable and with many of the topics generic to schools across the UK, they are well worth a look. Excellent.

National Library of Scotland: learning zone

www.nls.uk/learning-zone/history

This has learning resources for a range of historical events and topics related to Scottish history, including the Plague in Scotland and Women's Suffrage.

National Portrait Gallery: learning resources

www.npg.org.uk/learning/digital/history

Excellent learning resource from the National Portrait Gallery looking at how to read portraits as historical evidence. This has downloadable teacher resources for: Tudors; Abolition of Slavery; World War 1; Mary Seacole; and A Picture of Health: A Time of Medicine and Social Reform.

Primary school teaching ideas

www.teachingideas.co.uk/subjects/history

A huge collection of downloadable teaching resources, ideas and activities for KS1 and KS2 History. It includes: the Egyptians; Romans; Vikings; World War 1; World War 2; and Early Human history, along with many more. Excellent.

Show Me: history

www.show.me.uk/section/history

This has history games, videos, craft activities and curious or interesting objects to discover from collections. Excellent.

Simply School's Lancashire: learning resources

www.simplyschools.org.uk/lancashire/resources

This provides links for lesson plans, activities, games and information that can be used in the classroom or at home to support history topics. The links to further resources are general and not specific to Lancashire. Well worth a visit.

University of Cambridge Museums: Home Activities

www.museums.cam.ac.uk/activities

A wealth of fun activities linked to history topics including: Ancient Greeks, Romans; Ancient Egyptians; and Victorians.

By topic

Ancient civilisations

Ancient Egypt

Ancient Egypt

www.macclesfieldmuseums.co.uk/schools-ancient-egypt

Find out about Macclesfield Museum's collection of Ancient Egyptian artefacts with interactive videos and downloadable activities.

Ancient Egypt: history resources for KS2

www.theboxplymouth.com/schools/learning-resources/ancient-egypt

This learning resource from The Box, Plymouth, is designed for KS2. It explores the Ancient Egyptian collection looking at Life and Death in Egypt, covering gods, goddesses and sacred animals; animal mummies; inside a tomb; and the journey to the afterlife. It includes activities to do at home or in the classroom.

Ancient Egypt: learning resources

www.childrensuniversity.manchester.ac.uk/learning-activities/history/ancient-egypt/introduction

A learning resource designed for KS2 by the Children's University in Manchester and The Manchester Mummy Project with Professor Rosalie David OBE. This has a series of modules on aspects of Ancient Egypt including an Egyptian Timeline; Ancient Egyptian Gods; and Writing in Hieroglyphs, amongst others. Excellent.

Ancient Egyptians: activities

www.museumsworcestershire.org.uk/collections/activities

A downloadable learning resource to create Ancient Egyptian jewellery and hieroglyphs. Select from Activities based on the Curriculum.

Discover Ancient Egypt

https://brightonmuseums.org.uk/discover/make-learn/home-schooling

This learning resource is linked to Brighton and Hove Museum's collection and displays but offers some interesting work that can be adapted. Select Archaeology and Ancient History.

Mummification Activities

www.museumsandgalleries.leeds.gov.uk/virtual-visit/online-activities/activities-for-kids

Select Mummification for an interesting set of activities and videos about Ancient Egyptians.

Ancient Greece

Ancient Greece: learning resources

www.childrensuniversity.manchester.ac.uk/learning-activities/history/ancient-greece/introduction

A learning resource designed for KS2 from the Children's University in Manchester and the Classics and Ancient History Department at Manchester University. It has modules on Ancient Greece; Greek Religion and the Gods; the Ancient Olympics; the Greek Alphabet and Language; and more with the opportunity to test your knowledge.

The Mayan Civilisation

The Maya interactive KS2 activity pack

www.cadburyworld.co.uk/schools-and-groups/schools/resources

A great learning resource exploring the Mayan civilisation for KS2.

Anglo-Saxons and Vikings

Anglo-Saxons and Vikings resource pack

www.museums.norfolk.gov.uk/norwich-castle/learning/learning-at-home

Select Anglo-Saxons and Vikings Resource Pack for information and activities for KS2.

Anglo-Saxons, Vikings and Normans

www.natgeokids.com/teacher-category/anglo-saxons-vikings-normans

Fantastic learning resource from National Geographic Kids.

Anglo-Saxon riddles

https://cimuseums.org.uk/museumfromhome

A fun activity to add to Anglo-Saxon learning. Select Anglo-Saxon Riddles.

How to make Anglo-Saxon bread and Viking oat cakes

www.durhamcathedral.co.uk/learning/online-resources

Two simple activities from Durham Cathedral to support learning on Anglo-Saxon and Viking topics. Select from Get Creative at Home for downloadable instructions to make Viking oat cakes or Anglo-Saxon bread. A great way to bring history to life in the classroom or at home.

Jorvik Viking Centre

www.jorvikvikingcentre.co.uk/discover-from-home

A wealth of activities and downloads created by the Jorvik Learning Team on all aspects of Vikings, including Viking history and culture. Excellent.

Show Me: Vikings

www.show.me.uk/editorial/1168-where-to-see-the-vikings

Short exploration about the Vikings. Includes links to other museums and places related to the Vikings to find out more.

Vikings

https://vikings.mrdonn.org

This covers: Viking geography; family and daily life; Viking food and drink; religion and Norse gods and goddesses; Viking exploration and warriors; and Viking longboats. It has information and related activities to do in the classroom or at home. It also has links to further information from other reputable websites such as the BBC and the Smithsonian Museum. A very impressive resource for children, parents and teachers. Excellent.

Vikings: activities

www.chesterfield.gov.uk/explore-chesterfield/museum/more-from-your-museum/things-to-do/activities.aspx

Viking-themed activities to do at home or in the classroom. Select The Vikings.

Vikings – KS2

www.durhamcathedral.co.uk/learning/online-resources

Select Vikings - Key Stage 2. Learn about the Vikings with this downloadable resource from Durham Cathedral.

Archaeology

Archaeology: learning resources

www.liverpoolmuseums.org.uk/archaeology-learning-resources

This has four downloadable activity sheets looking at the archaeology of Merseyside. They include Prehistoric Merseyside; Roman Merseyside; Medieval Merseyside; and Industrial Merseyside.

Archaeology: pre-history

www.archaeologydataservice.ac.uk/learning/schoolsResources.xhtml

The Archaeology Data Service has resources specially selected for use in primary and secondary education that are great for teachers and parents to integrate into history or archaeology learning. The teaching and learning tools are divided into Primary Education for KS1 and KS2 covering topics on: Prehistory; Roman Britain; the Anglo-Saxons; the Vikings; and Ancient Egypt. Secondary Education for KS3 and KS4 covers topics on: Roman Britain; Medieval Britain; and Modern History. It is worth highlighting the *Prehistoric Burial Information Pack for Schools* focusing on prehistoric burial from Stone Age to Iron Age, which includes three specially commissioned poems by children's poet Michael Rosen, inspired by three real prehistoric burials. General information about Neolithic, the Bronze Age and the Iron Age across Britain is also given.

Archaeology quick reads

www.museumcrush.org/category/archaeology

Museum Crush offers a wealth of archaeology quick reads on some of the most curious and interesting archaeological finds, as well as reconstructions and reveals from x-ray investigations. It includes the only UK found Viking helmet; a Bronze-Age double-sided shaving razor from the Havering Hoard; and a rare relic of the Iron Age warrior, to name but three in the vast offering of archaeology finds and treasures. This is a must for children, parents and teachers who are interested in archaeology and its importance for understanding history and it should inspire those who may have never thought about archaeology until now. Excellent.

Black history

The Black Curriculum

www.theblackcurriculum.com

This is a social enterprise that aims to deliver black British history across the UK. It has a curriculum and some free resources to use to teach pupils about Black history.

Black British humanitarians

www.redcross.org.uk/get-involved/teaching-resources/celebrating-black-history-month

A fantastic resource from the British Red Cross for secondary pupils to discover some exceptional Black British humanitarians.

Black history: learning activities

www.childrensuniversity.manchester.ac.uk/learning-activities/history/black-history/introduction

This is a resource from the Ahmed Iqbal Ullah Race Relations Resource Centre and

Library at Manchester University, which contains material and information about Black history and Black people's struggle against racism. The online resource looks at some of the important Black figures and their contribution to history. Suitable for KS2 and KS3.

Black history: learning resources

https://hackney-museum.hackney.gov.uk/learning

These resources, although specifically for the London Borough of Hackney, have a lot of valuable content that can be used and adapted by students, teachers and educators from around the UK. With themes such as African and Caribbean hair and fashion, African fabrics and enslavement and abolition it is well worth a look. There are also short films on How Diaries Can Capture History; Not Just Hair; and African Threads.

Black history: Lord Constantine's story

https://learning.parliament.uk/en/resources/black-history-month-lord-constantines-story

Lord Constantine was the first black member of the House of Lords in 1969. Learn about how his achievements paved the way for change. This is a video resource suitable for KS2 and KS3.

Black history: resources for home schooling

www.liverpoolmuseums.org.uk/black-lives-matter

These are resources from the Colonial Countryside Project with the University of Leicester. It is aimed at Year 5 to Year 8. The project has been led by Miranda Kaufman who wrote *Black Tudors*. The lessons are designed to address a gap in knowledge about country houses' links to the British Empire. Scroll in Resources to Colonial Countryside.

Black history and heritage

www.blackculturalarchives.org/subject-guides

This provides subject guides to key themes, giving a historical overview using items in the Black Cultural Archives Collection. The timelines for each theme are very useful. This resource would benefit KS4 and KS5.

Black people in late 18th-century Britain

www.english-heritage.org.uk/visit/places/portchester-castle/history-and-stories/black-people-in-late-18th-century-britain

Investigates black people living in Britain during the 18th century.

Black prisoners of war at Portchester Castle

www.english-heritage.org.uk/visit/places/portchester-castle/history-and-stories/black-prisoners-at-portchester

The story of 2,500 black prisoners of war who left the Caribbean on fleets of ships in 1796 and ended up in Portchester Castle.

Black Star education

www2.bfi.org.uk/education-research/education/black-star-education

Using British film and TV titles, the British Film Institute learning resource explores race and representation on the screen. It is excellent for curriculum subjects for KS4 and KS5 including English, PSHE and Citizenship. The teaching resources have been developed by teachers and include lesson plans with resources and ideas that would be equally useful for home learning. Excellent.

Brent's Windrush Generation: West Indian front rooms, reggae and positivity

www.museumcrush.org/brents-windrush-generation-west-indian-front-rooms-reggae-and-inspiring-stories

Stories of life in the London Borough of Brent related to the Windrush generation.

Celebrating the lives of black sailors at The Old Royal Naval College

www.museumcrush.org/celebrating-the-lives-of-black-sailors-at-the-old-royal-naval-college

Find out the story of black sailors of the Royal Navy, at one time the largest employer of black labour.

Civil rights movement

www.nobelprize.org/nobel-prize-lessons-theme-martin-luther-king-jr-and-the-civil-rights-movement

A lesson plan from the Nobel Prize for use in the classroom on Martin Luther King Jr and the civil rights movement.

The civil rights movement in America 1945–1968

www.historylearningsite.co.uk/the-civil-rights-movement-in-america-1945-to-1968

This covers the American civil rights timeline and important events including Truman and civil rights, Rosa Parks, Martin Luther King, Malcolm X, black power and the Black Panthers among many others. Excellent.

Hidden histories

www.manchester.ac.uk/connect/teachers/teacher-events-resources/resources/hidden-histories

Explore a collection of academic resources about Britain's Black, Asian and Minority ethnic communities. Includes *David Olusoga in Conversation discussing making history in the age of* #Black Lives Matter.

The life of Nelson Mandela

www.culturestreet.org.uk/teachers/mandela/lesson_plan.pdf

A structured lesson plan that provides an in-depth investigation and exploration of Nelson Mandela and the apartheid era of South Africa.

Martin Luther King in the UK

https://research.ncl.ac.uk/martinlutherking/activities/mlkinuk

A brilliant and extensive downloadable resource designed and produced by Newcastle University. The resource pack has been created to inspire young people to think about the world they live in and how they can help bring about change. It is aimed at 7-16-year-olds (KS2-KS4) and includes lesson plans, handouts, worksheets, music recordings and presentations. Excellent.

Royal Mint: black history pack

www.royalmint.com/mintlings

Select Black History Pack for a substantial downloadable learning resource aimed at KS3.

Slave trade

www.dur.ac.uk/4schools/learningonline/secondaryonline

A fantastic set of resources to consider the slave trade and the struggle to end slavery. Select from Online Resources.

Slavery and abolition: KS3 and KS4 history resource

www.theboxplymouth.com/schools/learning-resources/transatlantic-slavery-and-abolition

This explores Plymouth's involvement with the transatlantic slave trade and its eventual abolition, through objects, documents and paintings. It is a useful resource for students studying black history.

Slavery and abolition: timeline

www.theboxplymouth.com/schools/learning-resources/transatlantic-slavery-and-abolition-timeline

The Box, Plymouth, provides an excellent and extensive timeline for transatlantic slavery and abolition.

Star lecture: David Olusoga

www.manchester.ac.uk/discover/events/star-lectures/archive-olusoga

This is the keynote lecture from the University of Manchester's Professor of Public History, David Olusoga, for KS3 and KS4 Black History Study Day, part of Black History Month 2019. Excellent.

Transatlantic slavery

www.liverpoolmuseums.org.uk/schools-and-groups-resources-transatlantic-slavery

The International Slavery Museum has produced online resources, videos and audio to study the history of the transatlantic slave trade.

Windrush: teaching resources

www.blackculturalarchives.org/learning/schools-programme

This is a clear and colourful online resource and presentation from the Black Cultural Archives that has been developed for teachers and families. Suitable for KS3. Excellent.

Windrush stories

www.bl.uk/windrush

Windrush stories online resource.

Windrush stories: teaching resource for primary

www.bl.uk/teaching-resources/windrush-stories-primary-creative-writing

Teaching resources from the British Library for primary creative writing and activities using histories, people and objects featured on the Windrush stories online resource. The use of archives, images, documents and articles is excellent.

Windrush stories: teaching resource for secondary

www.bl.uk/windrush/articles/windrush-stories-creative-writing-activities-secondary-students

Teaching resources form the British Library for secondary creative writing and activities using histories, people and objects featured on the Windrush stories online resource. The use of archives, images, documents and articles is excellent.

Castles and buildings

Avoncroft Museum: Online Resources

https://avoncroft.org.uk/online-resources

Avoncroft Museum is home to 30 historic buildings. It has an interesting set of downloadable resources for four different buildings - a 15th century town house, a 1946 prefab, a 1790 windmill and a 1576 Tudor timber framed building. An unusual learning resource which includes templates to create a model of each building and could be incorporated into looking at how people lived or looking at architectural changes.

Time traveller

www.cardiffcastle.com/time-traveller/home.htm

Learn about Cardiff Castle and the people who lived there. A simple but useful resource to show how the castle changed over periods of history from Romans and Celts, Normans and Medieval, and Victorians to World War 2. Children can choose a character and find out about how they lived at each period of history. A great resource for topics on castles.

English Civil War

The English Civil War and life in the 17th century

www.nationalcivilwarcentre.com/learningfromhome

Find out about life in the 17th century and the English Civil War with podcasts, films and writing, craft and quiz activities. Also, select Making History for downloadable instructions for related crafts and items, along with the Game Zone for related word searches. Select Learning at Home.

Family history

Exploring family history fact file

www.canalrivertrust.org.uk/explorers/resources

This resource from the Canal and River Trust aims to show children how different historical resources can be used to find out about the past. Select and download Exploring Family History Fact File from the list of titles.

Great Fire of London

The Great Fire of London 1666

www.stpauls.co.uk/learning-faith/schools-families/distance-learning

Select Great Fire of London Story Sheet and Learning from the Great Fire of London from the resources on The Rebuilding of a Cathedral. This is a short, colourful downloadable story sheet along with a learning activities sheet on the topic. It is linked to the rebuilding of the cathedral and is an excellent learning resource on the topic.

Gunpowder Plot

Gunpowder Plot: learning resources

www.hrp.org.uk

Historic Royal Palaces has a number of downloadable teacher packs and video resources covering the Gunpowder Plot and The Story of Guy Fawkes. Select Schools, then Learning Resources, then Topic Stuarts.

The Story of Guy Fawkes and the Gunpowder Plot

www.hrp.org.uk

A great resource from Historic Royal Palaces, with information, facts and colour images. Select History and Stories, then Stuart. Excellent.

History of Medicine

Florence Nightingale: activities

www.derbymuseumsfromhome.com/explore-and-discover

This has a few simple activities that could support topics on Florence Nightingale for younger children. It includes a word search and the interesting use of the famous painting *The Mission of Mercy* by Jerry Barrett from the National Portrait Gallery as a spot the difference. A great way to get children to look at the painting closely and to initiate discussion. Select Florence Nightingale.

Florence Nightingale: KS1 learning resources

www.museums.norfolk.gov.uk/norwich-castle/learning/trails-and-resources#teacher_resource_pack_ks1

Three resources on Florence Nightingale, including a worksheet to compare modern and Victorian hospital wards.

Florence Nightingale Museum: learning resources

www.florence-nightingale.co.uk/free-learning-resources

This has excellent learning resources for KS1 and KS2 looking at aspects of Florence Nightingale's life, especially the Family and School learning pack, which was made in collaboration with Guy's and St Thomas' NHS Foundation Trust. It includes worksheets and activities about the work of nurses and midwives and Florence Nightingale.

History of medicine

www.abpischools.org.uk/topic/history-of-medicine

This is an excellent resource from the Association of the British Pharmaceutical Industry. It covers the history of medicine starting with Prehistoric Medicine and is aimed at 14-16-year-olds.

King cholera: GCSE learning resources

www.medicalmuseum.org.uk/resources

This is a GCSE History lesson on cholera outbreaks in the 1800s produced by Worcester Medical Museums. The lesson includes a teacher's guide, student worksheet, sources and a presentation. Excellent.

Industrial Revolution

Black Country history at home

www.bclm.co.uk/history-at-home/history-at-home/1.htm

These are learning resources for KS1 and KS2 to use at home or in the classroom on the history of the Black Country during the Industrial Revolution. It includes an interactive powerpoint. Excellent.

Canal history

www.canalrivertrust.org.uk/enjoy-the-waterways/canal-history

Fascinating history of the 2,000 miles of UK canals from the Industrial Revolution to the present time. It includes a digitised archive of 22,000 images and 37,000 historic records.

Canals – how and why the canals were built

www.canalmuseum.org.uk/learning/learners

Find out about canals and why they were built with the London Canal Museum.

The Industrial Revolution in Wales

www.library.wales/services/education/learning-resources/the-industrial-revolution

This has maps and other information sources to support teaching the Industrial Revolution in Wales for KS2, KS3 and KS4.

National Coal Mining Museum: mining factsheets

www.ncm.org.uk/learning/learning-resources/mining-factsheets

These provide an introduction to the history of coal mining, looking at the working life of miners and the conditions, mining machinery and inventions and pit ponies. Use the image bank to download for use in the classroom or at home: **www.ncm.org.uk/learning/learning-resources**

Victorian mines

www.nationalminingmuseum.com/learning/learning-at-home-with-national-mining-museum-scotland

A learning resource from the National Mining Museum Scotland looking at mining during the Victorian times with activities to do at home. Look also at the Children in the Mine and The 1842 Royal Commission film at **www.nationalminingmuseum.com/further-resources**

Irish history

Belfast Exposed: photographs archive

www.belfastexposed.org

With over 1 million photographs that record political, cultural and social change in Northern Ireland, including The Troubles, this is an important resource for students studying Irish history or students of photography.

Maritime history (including pirates)

Grace O'Malley: the pirate queen of Ireland

www.rmg.co.uk/discover/explore/graceomalley

Find out about the most famous female pirate, Grace O'Malley. Also includes further resources for the topic of pirates.

Salcombe Museum: maritime history resources

www.salcombemuseum.org.uk/resources

Salcombe Museum has downloadable learning resources on a wealth of maritime history and includes a resource on Pirates and Privateers. It has related activities for young children to do at home or at school, all of which would be great for exploring the sea.

Local history

Local history

www.co-operativeheritage.coop/homeschooling-resources

This resource teaches children how to utilise Google maps and other online resources to learn more about the history of community buildings around them. Suitable for KS2 and KS3. Select CHT_Map_detectives_worksheet_for-KS2_homeschooling.pdf.

Local history: activities

www.chesterfield.gov.uk/explore-chesterfield/museum/more-from-your-museum/things-to-do/activities.aspx

Find out how to discover more about your own local history. Select Local History.

Local history study

www.culturestreet.org.uk/teachers/Local%20history/lesson_plan.pdf

A lesson plan for young people to start a local history study to explore and find evidence of past industries in their local town or city. Excellent for ideas and structure.

Southampton through time

www.seacitymuseum.co.uk/online-activities

A resource pack for teachers or for learning at home on Southampton's history. Select Southampton Through Time.

Medieval times and the Normans

1066 and the Norman Conquest

www.english-heritage.org.uk/learn/1066-and-the-norman-conquest

Packed with information about the Norman Conquest and the Battle of Hastings, including the weaponry and characters of 1066. Well worth looking at.

Medieval fun: family activities

www.historicenvironment.scot/learn/medieval-fun-for-families

A great set of resources from Historic Environment Scotland with downloadable instructions and activities to look at and explore different medieval jobs. Excellent.

Normans: learning resources

www.hrp.org.uk

Historic Royal Palaces has a number of downloadable PDF and video resources covering various aspects of the Normans. Select Schools, then Learning Resources, then Topic.

Shaking hands with the past

www.richardiiiexperience.com/learning/classroom-resources

This is a series of vodcasts for use by teachers, parents and children, showing medieval artefacts and explaining their use, construction and history.

Pilgrim Fathers and the Mayflower

Mayflower 400: activity pack

www.seacitymuseum.co.uk/online-activities

Select Mayflower 400 to find out about the voyage of the Mayflower in this activity pack from Sea City Museum in Southampton.

Mayflower 400: legend and legacy: teachers pack

www.theboxplymouth.com/schools/learning-resources/mayflower-400-legend-and-legacy-teacher-pack

This is a set of interesting resources for teachers and educators exploring the legend and legacy of the sailing of the *Mayflower* in 1620. These resources supported the commemorative exhibition for Mayflower 400 and were created by The Box, Plymouth in partnership with Wampanoag Native American Advisory Committee, along with the help of over 100 museums, libraries and archives across the UK, USA and the Netherlands. It explores the context for the sailing of the *Mayflower*, looks at the lives of its passengers and considers the legacy. Suitable for KS2, KS3 and KS4.

Prehistoric Britain

Stone Age, Bronze Age and Iron Age

About the Bronze Age

www.museumoflondon.org.uk/schools/learning-resources

Select About the Bronze Age for a short video for KS1 and KS2 on what is meant by the Bronze Age.

Ancient history: learning packs

https://brightonmuseums.org.uk/discover/make-learn/home-schooling

Learn about Brighton and Hove's earliest residents, from the Stone Age to Anglo-Saxons. These PDF learning packs are based on Brighton and Hove Museum displays and collections and are aimed at children learning at home or teachers looking for additional resources. Select Archaeology and Ancient History.

Bronze Age and Stone Age Essex

www.colchester.cimuseums.org.uk/learn/teacher-resources

The downloadable teacher notes resource is suitable for all educators and provides a timeline, links and recommended books to support the topic.

Bronze Age: Whitehorse Hill: learning resources

www.theboxplymouth.com/schools/learning-resources/prehistory-white-horse-hill-image-bank

This resource explores the objects found at the excavation of Whitehorse Hill, Dartmoor, where an undisturbed cremation burial from the early Bronze Age was uncovered in 2011. Suitable for KS2.

Iron Age Wales – gods and war

www.museum.wales/stfagans/learning/resources

This downloadable resource is available as an e-book, iBook or PDF and explores Iron Age Wales and the world of the Celts through the collections at the National Museum of Wales. Select Iron Age Wales - Gods and War or Iron Age Wales - Daily Life of Celts.

Prehistory: image bank

www.theboxplymouth.com/schools/learning-resources/prehistory-image-bank

Explore detailed images of objects from prehistory that were found in or near Plymouth. Suitable for KS2.

Stone Age

www.creswell-crags.org.uk/education/teaching-resources

This is a guide to the Stone Age with downloadable activities and resources for teachers and for home learning. Excellent.

Stone Age: activities

www.chesterfield.gov.uk/explore-chesterfield/museum/more-from-your-museum/things-to-do/activities.aspx

Discover more about life in the Stone Age with activities that include how to make a spear, identifying animal bones and using necklaces to trade with. Select Stone Age.

Stone Age: board games

www.creswell-crags.org.uk/education/crags-at-home-resources

Two themed board games have been created by Creswell Crags for the topics of the Ice Age and the Stone Age. They can be downloaded to print and play.

Stone Age, Bronze Age and Iron Age

https://archaeology.mrdonn.org/stone_bronze_ironage.html

Great site for children to find out about these ancient civilisations. It has information, links to further information and activities to explore the topic. Excellent.

Stone Age flint knapping

https://archaeology.mrdonn.org/stone_bronze_ironage.html
Select About the Bronze Age, then KS1 and KS2 to find out how Stone Age people made their tools.

Romans

Boudiccan Revolt

www.bosworthbattlefield.org.uk/learning-new/home-schooling-resources
This is a series of videos for KS1 and KS2 Roman Britain curriculum covering the Boudiccan Revolt, from the Bosworth Battlefield Heritage Centre.

Crafty Romans: activities

www.arbeiaromanfort.org.uk/learning/crafty-romans-from-our-collections-home
A cross-curricular resource for schools and home with activities for learning and understanding. There are further downloadable activities for families to use to explore Roman Britain from the Arbeia Roman Fort: **www.arbeiaromanfort.org.uk/learning/family-learning-activities** - includes Make a Roman Banquet, Make a Roman Head Pot and Learn about Life as a Roman Soldier.

Discover Roman treasure

www.museum.wales/roman/learning/resources
An excellent resource that gives information and definitions on Roman artefacts and everyday objects. You can click on the web link under the picture to access further detailed information and photographs of items in the National Roman Legion Museum's collection. Select Roman Collections Online.

Education in the Roman times

www.museum.wales/roman/learning/resources
Find out what education was like for Roman children. This is a downloadable iBook, e-book or PDF from the National Roman Legion Museum. Suitable for KS2. Select Roman School.

Medicine in the Roman world

www.museum.wales/roman/learning/resources
Discover the ways Romans tried to prevent disease, how they made medicines and what they used to perform operations. This is a downloadable iBook, eBook or PDF from the National Roman Legion Museum. Suitable for KS2. Select Lotions and Potions.

Roman Baths

www.romanbaths.co.uk/children-pages

Discover the history of the Roman Baths and find out about life in Roman times through games, stories and facts.

Roman rhythm

www.museum.wales/roman/learning/resources

This uses video from the National Roman Legion Museum to show replica Roman musical instruments being played. Suitable for KS2. Select Roman Rhythm.

Romans

www.grosvenormuseum.westcheshiremuseums.co.uk

Grosvenor Museum has created downloadable Roman-themed films and worksheets including one on the Roman Legionary Soldier. Select Schools.

Romans: activities

www.cimuseums.org.uk/museumfromhome

This has a great selection of fun activities to do at home or in the classroom to support finding out about the Romans, including Write like a Roman; Make a Roman Shield; Make a Roman Helmet; and Make a Roman Sword.

Romans: activities

www.vindolanda.com

Select Learn, then Families, for activity sheets and craft downloads on aspects of the Romans and Roman life from Vindolanda Charitable Trust.

Romans: activities

www.museumsworcestershire.org.uk/collections/activities

A downloadable learning resource to create Roman mosaics and Roman jewellery. Select from Activities based on the Curriculum.

Romans: activities

www.chesterfield.gov.uk/explore-chesterfield/museum/more-from-your-museum/things-to-do/activities.aspx

Discover more about Roman Britain. Use the activities to create your own offering for a Roman shrine and learn how to play games like a Roman. Select Roman Britain.

Romans: KS2 teacher resource pack

www.museums.norfolk.gov.uk/norwich-castle/learning/trails-and-resources#teacher_resource_pack_ks1

This is an extensive learning resource from Norwich Castle Museum and Art Gallery, with information and activities for KS2.

Romans: learning resources

www.colchester.cimuseums.org.uk/learn/teacher-resources

Extensive resources on Roman Colchester from Colchester and Ipswich Museums. They are aimed at KS2 7–11 years and cover Roman homes, towns, religion, entertainment and science. Select Learning from Home Romans.

Scottish history

Historic Environment Scotland: teaching resources

www.historicenvironment.scot/learn/learning-resources/teaching-resources

Select Themed Resources for a set of topics of Scottish history which includes: Investigating Historic Places & Events; Life in Medieval Scotland and Mary Queen of Scots. The resources include castles and the Jacobite risings. There are also Gaelic versions of online resources at **www.historicenvironment.scot/learn/learning-resources/gaelic-resources**.

Select Make and Create for creative resources that complement the themed resources and can be used at home or at school. There are also additional resources for families to use at home by selecting Medieval Fun for Families from the menu bar. Excellent.

Spanish flu

Florence Nightingale Museum: Spanish flu

www.florence-nightingale.co.uk/spanish-flu-nursing-during-historys-deadliest-pandemic

This is a great resource on a topic in history seldom given adequate attention. Its resonance in 2020 gives this resource particular importance. There is also a secondary resource pack to download that is packed with fascinating information and testimonials, along with an oral history film called 'Could we experience a similarly deadly pandemic today'? A brilliant resource and eerily significant.

Titanic

The Sinking of the Titanic: activity pack

www.seacitymuseum.co.uk/online-activities

Select Titanic Activity Pack for a great resource from Sea City Museum in Southampton. It looks at the sinking of RMS Titanic with activities. Aimed at KS2. Suitable for use in the classroom or at home.

Titanic: learning resources

www.liverpoolmuseums.org.uk/schools-and-groups-resources-titanic

Explore the history of the Titanic with this set of learning resources from Liverpool Museums. The resources include a useful timeline and a video on the role of Liverpool in the Titanic story.

Tudors

Kett's Rebellion 1549

www.museums.norfolk.gov.uk/norwich-castle/learning/learning-at-home

Select Kett's Rebellion 1549 for an extensive resource pack, including information and activities for KS2.

Tudors: activities

www.chesterfield.gov.uk/explore-chesterfield/museum/more-from-your-museum/things-to-do/activities.aspx

Tudor-themed activities to do at home or in the classroom. Select the Tudors.

Tudors: learning resources

www.hrp.org.uk

Historic Royal Palaces has a number of downloadable PDF and video resources covering various aspects of the Tudors. Select Schools, then Learning Resources, then Topic.

War of the Roses

www.bosworthbattlefield.org.uk/learning-new/home-schooling-resources

This has a range of resources from the Bosworth Battlefield Heritage Centre, including videos, challenges and information on the War of the Roses; the Battle of Bosworth; Richard III; and Henry Tudor.

Victorians

Life in the workhouse

www.museums.norfolk.gov.uk/gressenhall-farm-and-workhouse/whats-here/online-resources

Find out what life was like for those in the workhouse during Victorian times using the learning resources from Gressenhall Farm and Workhouse Museum. Select Lorina Bulwer or Moaning Martha.

Victorian lives

www.co-operativeheritage.coop/homeschooling-resources

A simple resource to teach KS1 about life in Rochdale in Victorian times but could be used for any part of the UK. It compares the lives of rich and poor and the homes they lived in, along with the lives of the children who worked in the mills. Select KS1 History CHT Home Schooling Worksheet.pdf

Victorian lives

www.macclesfieldmuseums.co.uk/victorians

Learn about the differences between modern school life, playing and food compared to the Victorian era.

Victorian Scarborough

www.scarboroughmuseumstrust.com/learning/victorian-scarborough

This is an extensive learning resource for use by teachers, parents and educators that includes notes, presentations and downloadable activities. Suitable for KS2. Lots of ideas to use for other parts of the UK.

Victorian seaside

www.scarboroughmuseumstrust.com/art-gallery-resources

A short resource on how to construct, colour and decorate a Victorian bathing machine. An additional fun element to use with the topic of Victorians or The Seaside.

Victorians: learning resources

www.braintreemuseum.co.uk/online-educational-resources

This includes downloadable learning resources from Braintree Museum covering Victorian schools, Victorian money and Victorian life. Select the Victorians.

Victorians: learning resources

www.hrp.org.uk

Historic Royal Palaces has a number of downloadable PDF and video resources covering various aspects of the Victorians. Select Schools, then Learning Resources, then Topic.

Victorians: learning resources

www.liverpoolmuseums.org.uk/schools-and-groups-resources-victorians

This has video and audio resources on the different experience of the wealthy and the poor during Victorian times.

Welsh history

Age of the Princes

www.museum.wales/stfagans/learning/resources

This is a joint project led by the National Museum of Wales, The National Library of Wales, The Royal Commission on the Ancient and Historical Monuments of Wales and CADW. It uses items from their collections to produce downloadable resources to support the curriculum in Wales. *Age of the Princes* covers six themes: The Overview (Wales 1063-1282); Evidence; Everyday Life; Castles and Courts; Welsh Rulers; and Conquest of Wales. An extensive resource for KS2 and KS3. Great for use in the classroom or at home. Select Age of the Princes. Excellent

CADW: Welsh history

www.cadw.gov.wales/learn

This has a wealth of resources on the history of Wales. Select Education for

Teaching Resources and Home Education Resources. The KS2 and KS3 education packs are excellent and look at: Castles; Neolithic and Prehistoric periods; Roman; and Victorian. There are also fun activities for exploration.

Women's history (including women's suffrage)

Challenging notions of womanhood: The Pit Brow Lasses of the Northern Coalfields

www.museumcrush.org/challenging-notions-of-womanhood-the-pit-brow-lasses-of-the-northern-coalfields

The little-known social history of the women who worked in the coal industry. Excellent for inclusion in projects or learning looking at female equality or women at work.

Emily Wilding Davison: presentation

https://learning.parliament.uk/en/resources/emily-wilding-davison-primary-lesson-plan

Find out about Emily Wilding Davison who campaigned for equal rights for women during the Votes for Women campaign. The presentation links to the curriculum for all four nations and is suitable for KS1 and KS2. Available in Welsh.

History of Suffrage Vote 100: The Moving Story toolkit for schools

www.womenslibrary.org.uk/discover-our-projects/vote-100-the-moving-story/vote-100-toolkit-for-schools

Vote 100: The Moving Story was developed by the Glasgow Women's Library for the 100th anniversary of the Representation of the People Act. The toolkit supports Vote 100, offering activities for research, debate, creative writing and arts to engage 14-16-year-olds. It includes an animated resource to highlight those who campaigned for women to have the right to vote. Excellent.

The role of British women

www.historylearningsite.co.uk/the-role-of-british-women-in-the-twentieth-century

A fantastic resource covering the suffragette movement, significant people and events for women's rights and the role of women in World War 1 and World War 2.

Suffrage Rally

www.beamish.org.uk/learning/learning-resources

These resources for KS3 and KS4 look at the suffrage movement. It uses role play and drama to enable pupils to explore and gain understanding of the various arguments and groups who were for and against the movement. Although designed around a visit to the Beamish Museum, the resource still has value used independently within the classroom or at home.

Votes for women

www.culturestreet.org.uk/teachers/Votes_for_women/lesson_plan.pdf

A structured lesson plan packed with ideas to explore the struggle for equal rights for women.

Votes for women: learning resources

www.phm.org.uk/learn/ideas-worth-exploring/resources-votes-for-women

These are KS3 resources from the People's History Museum to support learning on Women's Suffrage 1900-1918 and the impact on women's rights and equality, along with finding out more about the campaign for women to have the right to vote in Britain. Excellent.

Votes for women: video and resource pack

https://learning.parliament.uk/en/resources/votes-for-women-video-and-resources

An excellent resource suitable for KS2 and KS3, using an audio drama following suffragette Lady Constance Lytton as she protests for women's right to vote. It has a lesson plan, which is available in English and Welsh. Great for use in the classroom or at home.

Welsh women's history 1900–1918

www.museum.wales/welsh_womens_history

This downloadable pack presents visual, oral and written resources dealing with women's experiences between 1900-1918.

Women, football and society

www.padlet.com/nfmcommunities

A fantastic set of resources exploring through photographs, video footage and documents the pioneers of women's football and its development.

Women's suffrage

www.nls.uk/learning-zone/history

This is a learning resource for secondary pupils on the women's suffrage movement in Scotland using material from the National Library of Scotland. It has been developed by teachers and is suitable for both school and home learning with a range of interesting materials.

Women's suffrage

www.show.me.uk/editorial/2348-topic-guide-women-s-suffrage

A great topic guide on women's suffrage with links to further information and visuals.

Women wearing the trousers – the archive of women striding across history

www.museumcrush.org/women-wearing-the-trousers-the-archive-celebrating-women-taking-strides-across-history

This is a fascinating look at the story of 'trouser-wearing women' from the 1850s to the 1960s and the role of 'wearing the trousers' in social and political change and women's liberation.

World War 1

Casualty Cleaning Station board game

www.medicalmuseum.org.uk/boardgame

This is a downloadable board game designed and produced by Worcester Medical Museums, based on the World War 1 scenario of a casualty evacuation chain manned by troops of the Royal Army Medical Corps. In playing the game, KS3 Maths students apply their knowledge of probabilities and percentages to choose the correct course of medical treatment for sets of injured solders. This is a unique resource for KS3 and KS4 to engage with history and maths.

The Greater Game: football and World War 1

https://padlet.com/nfmcommunities

A fantastic resource about the role and importance of football during World War 1. This includes the excellent activity pack and presentation from the British Council on the 1914 Christmas Truce. Select the Greater Game.

Imperial War Museum: learning resources

www.iwm.org.uk/learning/resources

Select either First World War or Second World War. This has fantastic learning resources from the Imperial War Museum, combining resources used with schools and those created for the Home Learning Hub. They include the Adventures in History resources and Family Mission activities, which were designed for families to gain skills while having history-related fun.

Incredible Journeys

www.storymuseum.org.uk/schools-groups/learning-resources

Incredible Journeys is a learning resource created by the Story Museum, Oxford, to support World War 1 learning. It tells the stories of World War 1 using animals from all round the world. There are downloadable lesson packs for each story providing background context and teaching ideas to use either at home or in the classroom. Suitable for KS2 and KS3. Excellent.

Last Post: the postal service in World War 1

www.postalmuseum.org/visit-us/schools/learning-resources/last-post

An excellent and interesting learning resource for KS1 and KS2 World War 1 topic looking at the importance of the postal service in war time. It uses archive documents, including photographs, maps and letters, as part of designed lesson plans, teachers' notes, activity ideas and powerpoint presentations.

Munitions worker: Annie Bullock

www.dormanmuseum.co.uk

Find out about the life of a munitions worker during World War 1. Select Local Hero: Annie Bullock.

National Library of Wales: World War 1

www.library.wales/services/education/learning-resources/the-first-world-war

These resources were produced as part of a joint project between the NLW and the National Museum of Wales to commemorate the centenary of World War 1 in Wales. The resources include lesson plans, videos, activities and detailed packs. Excellent.

Scotland and World War 1

www.nms.ac.uk/explore-our-collections/resources/for-teachers-secondary-resources

Explore the stories behind those who fought in World War 1 through a selection of keepsakes and objects from the National Museums Scotland. Select First World War.

Scouts during the wars

www.scouts.org.uk/supporters/remembrance/scouts-during-the-wars

A fascinating and interesting set of resources using personal stories, poetry and pictures to look at World War 1. Excellent.

Tank Museum: World War 1 & World War 2 activities

www.tankmuseum.org/services/school-trips/education-resources

This has a range of downloadable activities for teachers and parents to use to support history topics on World War 1 and World War 2.

The Unknown Warrior: a four-minute film

www.westminster-abbey.org/teaching-resources/the-unknown-warrior-a-four-minute-film

Uncover the story behind the Grave of the Unknown Warrior with this short film along with downloadable resources. It is suitable for primary and secondary and for those learning at home.

Women in the Great War

www.nls.uk/learning-zone/history

Learn about women's role in World War 1 using archive material from the National Library of Scotland collections. It has learning materials on various roles women had, including as ambulance drivers on the Western Front and working in France and Romania. A great resource for secondary pupils. Select Women in the Great War.

World War 1: centenary resource

www.redcross.org.uk/get-involved/teaching-resources/world-war-one-centenary-resource

An extensive teaching package from the British Red Cross that uses the digitised archive and original source material from World War 1. Suitable for 11-16 years to look at the role volunteers played in the war. Excellent.

World War 1 and World War 2

www.natgeokids.com/teacher-category/significant-events

Downloadable activity sheets for teachers and parents. Suitable for KS1 and KS2.

World War 1

www.parliament.uk/about/living-heritage/transformingsociety/parliament-and-the-first-world-war

A wealth of learning resources and information, including video and archive images, to explore World War 1. Excellent.

World War 1: secondary school resources

www.dur.ac.uk/4schools/learningonline/secondaryonline

A fantastic set of resources to consider what it was like to fight in World War 1, trench warfare and the impact of new technology.

World War 1: The autograph books of the 'Gretna Girls' munitions workers

www.museumcrush.org/the-autograph-books-of-the-gretna-girls-munitions-workers

This is so interesting and well worth looking at when considering the role of women in World War 1.

World War 1 Local Hero: Tom Dresser activity pack

www.dormanmuseum.co.uk

Find out about local hero Tom Dresser from Middlesbrough, a soldier in World War 1 who successfully crossed No Man's Land to get help for much needed ammunition. Includes activities about the war.

World War 1 and Parliament: video and resource pack

https://learning.parliament.uk/en/resources/world-war-one-and-parliament

Using videos, including two re-enacted speeches, this explores the role of Parliament in the outbreak of World War 1. It links to the curriculums of the four nations and includes a downloadable lesson pack for KS3 and KS4. Select Resources and then UK Parliament and World War 1. Excellent.

World War 2 and the Holocaust

Anne Frank: writing in impossible circumstances

www.amnesty.org.uk/resources/lessons-writing-impossible-circumstances

Two downloadable lessons produced by Amnesty International and the Anne Frank Trust to explore Anne Frank's life and legacy through the context of the right to freedom of expression and opinion. It includes a powerpoint, resource sheets and teacher notes. Excellent.

Battle of Britain Bunker: World War 2

www.battleofbritainbunker.co.uk/virtual-resources

This has a selection of downloadable resources covering various aspects of World War 2. Suitable for KS2 and KS3. It includes the Role of Women, the Little Ships in the Dunkirk Evacuation and Operation Dynamo.

Billy Brown of London Town

www.ltmuseum.co.uk/visit/families/family-activities/billy-brown-london-town

A fun set of activities around the character of Billy Brown, who helped passengers during World War 2 know what to do and what not to do in the London Underground.

Bletchley Park: VE Day learning resources

www.bletchleypark.org.uk/learn/resources/ve-day-learning-resources

This includes an excellent VE Day Celebration Pack, along with VE Day activities and colouring sheets.

The Blitz

www.stpauls.co.uk/learning-faith/schools-families/distance-learning

Select St Paul's during the Blitz for an excellent and interesting curriculum-based set of resources on the story of St Paul's during the Blitz, plus the stories of the volunteers and bomb disposal squad involved in saving the cathedral. It includes footage of the removal of the bomb. Excellent for showing the impact of the Blitz and has lots of suggested activities. In addition, there is another interesting story about the cathedral cat, Faith, who was given a medal for bravery. Scroll down and select Faith the Cat.

The Boy in the Striped Pyjamas

www.filmeducation.org/theboyinthestripedpyjamas

These are Film Education resources to support the film and its use in World War 2 history study.

Courageous animals

https://cdn.faber.co.uk/media/wysiwyg/Final_Heroes_Resource_Pack_small.pdf

This is a resource pack for KS2 teachers using one story from the book *Heroes: Incredible Stories of Courageous Animals* by David Long. It could be equally used at home to link to World War 2 themes and projects on animals. Access to the resource and the story used - 'Voyteck: The Bear Who Carried Bombs' - can also be found by using **www.faber.co.uk/faber-childrens-resources** and scrolling down the list of children's books offered from Faber with learning resources.

D-Day timeline

www.theddaystory.com/d-day-timeline

Excellent timeline on the journey to D-Day.

Eden Camp: World War 2

www.edencamp.co.uk/schools/isolation-home-activities

This has a set of downloadable activities related to World War 2, which includes Build Your Own Andersen Air Raid Shelter and Wartime Recipes. Great for bringing the topic to life.

The Holocaust explained

www.theholocaustexplained.org

The website has been created by the Wiener Holocaust Library, based in London since 1933 and the oldest archive of Holocaust materials. It has been created to help children and young people understand the facts of the Holocaust, its cause and its consequences. It is designed for the school curriculum for 13-18-year-olds and is organised into nine topic areas. Excellent.

The Holocaust through art: The Ben Uri Collection: for GCSE studies

www.benuri.org/schoolsandfamilies

This programme is designed to help students deconstruct the relevant works of the Ben Uri Collection in order to be a stimulus for their own understanding of the period. As a result, they will gain an insight into pre- and post-war life in Central Europe, artists and their subject matter. There are 15 discussion sheets on 15 artworks with an overview of the artist, discussion on the composition, materials, content and ideas. There are an additional five activity packs to explore with all documents and images available to download. The resource is suitable for supporting Holocaust studies for GCSE History. Excellent.

Jewish Museum: learning resources: Jewish history and the Holocaust

www.jewishmuseum.org.uk/schools/in-the-classroom

This has extensive resources for use in the classroom or at home covering KS1 to A Level. Search by resource type, key stage or by area of study, which includes During

War '39–'45; Pre-War '33–'39; Immigration and Migration; and many more. Select Curriculum then History or Holocaust (or both) for a wealth of resources on aspects of Jewish history and the Holocaust. Excellent.

Money during World War 2

www.tankmuseum.org/wp-content/uploads/2020/04/Old-Money-Maths-KS2.pdf

An old money maths activity from the Tank Museum.

National Library of Wales: World War 2

www.library.wales/services/education/learning-resources/the-second-world-war

The resources from the NLW on World War 2 look at Welsh people's experiences during the war with resources divided into two packs. One pack covers KS1 and KS2 with the themes of Children's Experiences, including Evacuees; the Home Front; Rationing; and Remembrance. For KS3 and KS4, the resources cover Children's Lives during World War 2; Women's Lives during World War 2; and the Home Front, along with specific key Welsh figures - David Lloyd George and Gareth Vaughan Jones.

Northern Ireland War Memorial Museum: learning resources

www.niwarmemorial.org/learning-resources

A great set of learning resources to use at home or in the classroom. It includes downloadable instructions for making wartime toys; template and instructions for making a ration book and a National Identity Card, along with wartime ration recipes and VE Day activities and Victory Songbook. Excellent.

Radar and Bernard Lovell

www.jodrellbank.net/ve-day

Explore Bernard Lovell's role in World War 2 and how his pioneering work developing the H25 airborne radar system proved decisive in the outcome of the war. Also learn about radar and discover how wartime developments in radar technology later helped scientists make achievements in astronomy.

Royal Air Force: World War 1 and World War 2

www.raf100schools.org.uk

The Historical Association and the Institute of Physics have created this fantastic resource combining history and STEM. The films, activities and resources provide innovative ways of exploring scientific ideas and their history in connection to the RAF. It includes downloadable resources on The Battle of Britain and radar.

Scotland and World War 2

www.nms.ac.uk/explore-our-collections/resources/for-teachers-secondary-resources

Discover Scottish stories related to different aspects of World War 2: life on the Home

Front; the development of technology driven by the conflict; and personal memories of those who lived through the time.

Secret art of survival: family resource pack

www.vgm.liverpool.ac.uk/schools-families-and-home/vgmathomefamily

The Victoria Gallery & Museum in Liverpool has activities inspired by a hidden piece of World War 2 history. Thousands of allied servicemen became prisoners of the Japanese known as Far East Prisoners of War (FEPOW) and used art to secretly record their experiences.

Silk escape maps

https://macclesfieldmuseums.co.uk/world-war-ii

Find out about the World War 2 silk escape maps and Morse Code from Macclesfield Museums.

VE Day

www.discoverymuseum.org.uk/week-3-ve-day

A selection of simple World War 2 downloadable activities to do at home or in the classroom related to VE Day.

Wartime Britain 1940s

https://film.britishcouncil.org/resources/film-archive

Explore over 100 short documentaries about wartime Britain made during the 1940s. Excellent for supporting history learning and curiosity.

World War 2: activities

www.chesterfield.gov.uk/explore-chesterfield/museum/more-from-your-museum/things-to-do/activities.aspx

World War 2-themed activities to do at home or in the classroom. They include an Andersen Shelter template; Making a Gas Mask; and themed activities for VE Day. Select World War 2.

World War 2: codebreakers

www.raf100schools.org.uk/activity/36/3-codebreakers-communication

Explore the role and impact of secret messages and codebreaking in World War 2.

World War 2: Home Front

www.blackburnmuseum.org.uk/learning/ww2-short-films

A series of short films exploring the realities of life in Blackburn and Darwen during World War 2. These look at rationing and the black out.

World War 2: learning resources

www.culturenl.co.uk/museums/learning-museums

This has a number of resources about World War 2 including: Jobs for Civilians; Reserved Occupations; 1940s House & Garden; Code Breaking; and Rationing. Select Learning at Home, then Museums at Home, then Second World War.

World War 2: learning resources

www.parliament.uk/about/living-heritage/transformingsociety/parliament-second-world-war

A wealth of learning resources and information including video and archive images to explore World War 2. Excellent.

World War 2: the shrapnel-riddled jacket that tells the story of the RAF at Dunkirk

www.museumcrush.org/the-shrapnel-riddled-jacket-that-tells-the-story-of-the-raf-at-dunkirk

The Imperial War Museum tells the story of a bullet-riddled jacket of a pilot shot down during the evacuation of Dunkirk and the impact of the biggest military evacuation in history - Operation Dynamo.

World War 2 and Parliament

https://learning-parliament.uk

A great downloadable resource and video to explore the role of Parliament in World War 2. Select Resources and then UK Parliament and World War II for Secondary or for Primary. This resource is available in Welsh. Excellent.

C ICT

See also: Health and wellbeing – Online safety

ICT is, of course, continually evolving. The learning resources below include some of the popular programs and software used currently within ICT learning, especially related to coding. There are also some historical resources to highlight the development of the computer and the information connected world.

Information

Colossus: the world's first electronic computer

www.tnmoc.org/galleries

Find out about Colossus, the world's first electronic computer, and the Electronic Random Number Indicator Equipment (ERNIE), along with Programmable Machines; Computer Languages; Personal Computers; and much more. In addition, there are also excellent Computing Challenges, divided into Word Challenges, Picture Challenges and Heritage Challenges.

Computing history timeline

www.computinghistory.org.uk/cgi/computing-timeline.pl

The computing timeline covers from 0001 to the present day. Fascinating detail for every important date.

Learning resources and activities

For primary

Barclays Code Playground

www.scienceoxford.com/resources/science-oxford-recommends/code-playground

Suitable for 7–12-year-olds to have fun while learning the basics of coding in Scratch, with further videos to find out other techniques to use.

Codebreakers and communications

www.raf100schools.org.uk/activity/36/3-codebreakers-communication

A downloadable STEM activity for children and young people to build a communication circuit and a scrambler to use to send encoded and encrypted messages.

Computing: learning resources

www.computinghistory.org.uk

The Centre for Computing History has a fantastic set of downloadable guides for a host of computer programming and related topics including Build Your Own Website; Geometric Patterns using Python Turtle; Introduction to Raspberry Pi;

Introduction to Python with Raspberry Pi: Pixel Sprites; Create a Video Game Character; and many more. Suitable for KS2 and KS3. Select Education, then Learning. Excellent.

Cracking code breakers

www.postalmuseum.org/visit-us/schools/learning-resources

Select Cracking Code Breakers for a learning resource aimed at KS2 looking at the story of early computing. This would be great too for KS3, covering the story of Colossus and codebreaking. It includes student challenges, teachers notes, film clips and powerpoints.

ICT: KS1

www.teachcomputing.org/home-teaching/key-stage-1

These are resources from the National Centre for Computer Education, which are to be used with parents for home learning or within the classroom with teachers.

ICT: KS2

www.teachcomputing.org/home-teaching/key-stage-2

These are resources from the National Centre for Computer Education, which are to be used with parents for home learning or within the classroom with teachers. The downloadable resources are from the Raspberry Pi Foundation.

Primary computing resources

www.stem.org.uk/primary-computing-resources

Excellent primary computing resources to support the curriculum and to use at home. It covers Algorithms; Data; Digital Literacy; Information Technology; and Programming.

Primary school teaching ideas

www.teachingideas.co.uk/subjects/computing

Teaching ideas and resources for ICT for KS1 and KS2.

Royal Signals Museum: exploring communications activities

www.royalsignalsmuseum.co.uk/activities

These are activities with downloadable instructions to explore the world of communications. They include creating your own electric car, a tin can communicator and a code wheel.

World Wide Web primary resources

www.natgeokids.com/uk/teacher-category/technology

A downloadable resource from National Geographic Kids, looking at the development of the World Wide Web and its founder Tim Berners-Lee. Select World Wide Web Primary Resources.

For secondary

Codebreakers and communication

www.raf100schools.org.uk/activity/36/3-codebreakers-communication

A downloadable STEM activity for children and young people to build a communication circuit and a scrambler to use to send encoded and encrypted messages.

ICT: KS3

www.teachcomputing.org/home-teaching/key-stage-3

These are resources from the National Centre for Computer Education, which are to be used with parents for home learning or within the classroom with teachers. Topics included are Digital Literacy; App Development; Cyber Security; and Python Programming.

ICT: KS4

www.teachcomputing.org/home-teaching/key-stage-4

These are resources from the National Centre for Computer Education, which are to be used with parents for home learning or within the classroom with teachers. Topics included are Python Programming; Maths & Logic in Computer Science; and Object Orientated Programming.

ICT: KS5

www.teachcomputing.org/home-teaching/key-stage-5

These are resources from the National Centre for Computer Education, which are to be used with parents for home learning or within the classroom with teachers. This covers Object Orientated Programming with resources from Future Learn.

National Museum of Computing: remote learning packages

www.tnmoc.org/remote-learning-packages

This has learning resources for Cospaces, Beebem (BBC Micro Emulator), Trinket and RiveScript.

National Videogame Museum: learning resources

www.thenvm.org/learning/learn-at-home

A fantastic set of resources developed with the University of Sheffield to learn how to make computer games. It includes Getting Started with Pixel Art; Getting Started with Scratch; Getting Started with Twine; and Getting Started with Bitsy. Suitable for KS2 and KS3.

STEM Learning: secondary and A Level computing resources

www.stem.org.uk/secondary-alevel-computing

Fantastic resources for KS3 and A Level computing, covering Algorithms; Data; Digital Literacy; Information Technology; Programming; and much more. To access the resources, you are required to complete the free registration.

INVENTIONS AND DISCOVERIES

Inventors, inventions and discoveries are all part of STEM learning and development. The great inventors, engineers and scientists, along with their inventions and discoveries, have inspired and shaped our world and showcase the importance and impact STEM has on all our lives.

Information

How products are made

www.madehow.com

This is as wonderful and comprehensive a list of products and how they are made, including their history, as you can find. It is arranged alphabetically. US website.

Inventions 1900 to 1990

www.historylearningsite.co.uk/inventions-and-discoveries-of-the-twentieth-century/inventions-1900-to-1990

Inventor archive

https://lemelson.mit.edu/resources/inventor-archive

No list can ever be considered exhaustive but this A–Z of inventors makes a good attempt at listing inventors from around the world and providing an overview of their main contributions.

Inventors and scientists

www.ducksters.com/biography

Select Inventors and Scientists. A good starting point.

Inventors and what they invented

www.design-technology.info/inventors

This is a list of inventors and what they invented. Select from the list to find out more. A good starting point.

Technology at home

www.pbs.org/wgbh/aso/tryit/tech/index-nojs.html

Find out how technological inventions have transformed our homes. Then find out about the people behind each of the inventions and how it works.

Learning resources and activities

Inventions and innovations

www.sciencemuseum.org.uk/learning

Select Resources for the Classroom. There are a number of inventions and innovations available within this learning resource, including the Enigma Cipher Machine.

Inventors and inventions: short films

www.blackburnmuseum.org.uk/learning/short-films-for-schools

This is a series of short films by Blackburn Museum and Art Gallery aimed at KS2 pupils for the topic of Inventors and Inventions. It includes The Phonograph; The Biro; The Eggbox; The Top Hat; and Polypropylene. Intriguing.

National Inventors Hall of Fame

www.invent.org/at-home-learning-resources

In the spirit of invention, this site offers a wealth of home activities to encourage STEM activity. Although an American site, many of the activities are relevant to UK learning. The downloadable STEM guide gives one-page activities and highlights the inventor that has inspired the activity. This is an excellent model to bring STEM subjects to life and relate to those who have invented or discovered.

Thomas Edison: Victorian inventor

www.show.me.uk/editorial/1177-thomas-edison-victorian-inventor

Short exploration of the life of Thomas Edison with links to find out more.

World Wide Web primary resources

www.natgeokids.com/uk/teacher-category/technology

A downloadable resource from National Geographic Kids looking at the development of the World Wide Web and its founder Tim Berners-Lee. Select World Wide Web Primary Resources.

Black inventors

The A–Z list of Black inventors

www.interestingengineering.com/the-a-z-list-of-black-inventors

An A–Z list of Black and African-American inventors. This is a fascinating list, thanks to Henry Baker who worked in the US Patent Office in the 1800s and early 1900s. He wanted African-Americans, who had few rights at the time, to receive some form of recognition for their contribution to inventions and devised a unique mark on the forms of African-Americans who submitted patents to the US Patent Office. This left a unique legacy in the form of a record of African-American contribution to society and the world.

Discoveries and explorers

Beyond endurance: Antarctica, Ernest Shackleton and James Wordie

www.nls.uk/learning-zone/geography-and-exploration

Find out the story of the Trans-Antarctic Expedition 1914-1917 with Ernest Shackleton and James Wordie. Select Shackleton and Wordie.

Captain Cook

www.dormanmuseum.co.uk/learning/captain-cook-birthplace-museum-education-resource-pack

This is an education pack for use in the classroom or at home on the life and adventures of Captain James Cook. It is divided into three downloadable sections covering Early Life; Life at Sea; and Places Cook Visited.

Sir Francis Drake and the circumnavigation of the globe

https://community.dur.ac.uk/4schools.resources/Drake/default.htm

An interesting resource for pupils using historical documents to question whether Sir Francis Drake embarked on a Voyage of Discovery or a Voyage of Plunder.

Women inventors

Women inventors

www.factmonster.com

For a fun list of child-related items invented by women, select People, then Women of Influence, followed by Mothers of Invention. It is American but most items are recognisable.

Famous women inventors

www.women-inventors.com

The women listed are all American inventors, nevertheless, a host of amazing inventions that are either household items or names.

51 female inventors

www.interestingengineering.com/female-inventors-and-their-inventions-that-changed-the-world-and-impacted-the-history-in-a-revolutionary-way

An extensive resource offering a wealth of information on each of the 51 female inventors, scientists and engineers listed. It does require scrolling through but well worth it.

C MATHS

There are two basic things that are useful for maths learning, one is the method and the other is practice. The resources given below provide lots of knowhow and heaps of activities for practice and application. Many of the organisations provide downloadable worksheets, which are invaluable for home learning and can be repeated until mathematical perfection is achieved - some even make the process enjoyable!

Learning resources and activities

Cambridge University NRICH: mathematical resources

www.nrich.maths.org

NRICH is a collaboration between the Faculties of Mathematics and Education at the University of Cambridge. It provides free online maths resources for 3-18-year-olds, with the aim to develop mathematical thinking and problem-solving while offering inspiring and engaging activities. There are sections for Primary Students; Secondary Students; Early Years; Primary Teachers; and Secondary Teachers. This is an extensive resource for all - including teachers and those home learning. Excellent.

Mathematics Education Innovation (MEI): free resources

https://mei.org.uk/free-resources

MEI has an extensive range of downloadable resources and materials available for young people, parents and teachers to support maths learning.

National Geographic Kids: primary maths resources

www.natgeokids.com/uk/teacher-category/maths

This covers counting; games; geometry and measuring.

Oxford Owl for Home: maths

https://home.oxfordowl.co.uk/maths

A wonderful and extensive learning resource from Oxford University Press for children from 5-11 years covering Addition & Subtraction; Multiplication & Division; Fractions; and Geometry & Shapes. There are plenty of tips for parents to help their children with maths and in addition there's a maths glossary to help or remind parents about the terminology used in maths.

Primary Mathematics Challenge

www.primarymathschallenge.org.uk

The Primary Mathematics Challenge is an annual mathematical challenge aimed at pupils of primary age, including schools and home schooling. It has past maths papers to download to use as practice before the Challenge. These include the answers and notes. Not only are the papers useful for aspiring mathematicians signing up to the Challenge but also fantastic for home use and as a learning resource. The Challenge is run by the Mathematical Association. Every week it sets a question for children to attempt and gives the solution later in the week.

Science Museum: have fun with maths

https://learning.sciencemuseumgroup.org.uk/learning-resources

Learn about maths concepts with the Science Museum using activities, image banks and 3D objects. Excellent.

For primary

Dad's worksheets

www.dadsworksheets.com

This US site has an extensive collection of printable worksheets, online calculators, games, puzzles and tools related to maths. It covers Core Maths; Fractions; Percentages; Measurements; and Number Patterns.

Mathematics mastery: Early Years & Key Stage 1–2 resources

www.arkcurriculumplus.org.uk/home-learning-support/eyfs-and-ks1-2-resources

This has downloadable resource packs for Reception, KS1 and KS2. Select Early Years and KS1, then Reception, Y1 or Y2, then Maths or Key Stage 2, then either Y3, Y4, Y5 or Y6, then Maths. These are great resources to use at home or in the classroom.

Maths on toast: the family maths charity

www.mathsontoast.org.uk/fun-maths-at-home

This has fun activities and resources including family games that can bring fun into maths learning at home.

Maths resources for home learning: primary

www.stem.org.uk/home-learning/primary#maths

This has extensive resources to support maths learning at home. To access the resources, you are required to complete the free registration. Excellent.

Money during World War 2

www.tankmuseum.org/wp-content/uploads/2020/04/Old-Money-Maths-KS2.pdf

An old money maths activity from the Tank Museum.

Murderous Maths

www.murderousmaths.co.uk

The official Murderous Maths website created by Kjartan Poskitt. This is packed with fun activities and games all related to maths with teacher/parent resources, number tricks and puzzles. There are printable resource sheets. Great fun and well worth looking at.

Numeracy Family Maths Toolkit

www.familymathstoolkit.org.uk

This has ideas to help parents, families and children aged 13 and under to enjoy everyday maths activities together. It also offers resources to help teachers support family engagement with children's maths learning.

Primary mathematics resources

www.stem.org.uk/primary-maths

This includes resources on topics such as Number and Place Value; Addition and Subtraction; Multiplication and Division; Fractions; Decimals and Percentages; Measures; Geometry; Data & Statistics; and Algebra. To access the resources, you are required to complete the free registration. Excellent.

Primary school teaching ideas

www.teachingideas.co.uk

Select Maths for a host of teaching ideas and resources covering KS1 and KS2 maths. It includes Problem Solving; Money; Algebra; Geometry; Measurements; and Statistics, all with downloadable activity sheets. Excellent for use in the classroom or at home.

Roald Dahl: create and learn

www.roalddahl.com/create-and-learn

Select Lesson Plans for Titchy Toddlers for a pre-school numeracy activity called *Start Counting with Croc!* Could be used with Reception and KS1 children.

Shopping maths activity

www.co-operativeheritage.coop/homeschooling-resources

A simple well-produced KS1 maths activity using the Co-operative Heritage Trust store history to develop maths skills. Select CHT Maths KS1 Shopping with the Pioneers.

Time and sport

www.olympic.org/museum/visit/schools/teaching-resources/support-de-cours/time-and-sport

A series of information and activity sheets to explore measuring time.

For secondary

Casualty Cleaning Station board game

www.medicalmuseum.org.uk/boardgame

This is a downloadable board game designed and produced by Worcester Medical Museums, based on the World War 1 scenario of a casualty evacuation chain manned by troops of the Royal Army Medical Corps. In playing the game, KS3 maths students apply their knowledge of probabilities and percentages to choose the correct course of medical treatment for sets of injured solders. This is a unique resource for KS3 and KS4 to engage with history and maths.

Mathematics mastery: KS3 resources

www.arkcurriculumplus.org.uk/home-learning/ks3-resources

This has downloadable resource packs for KS3. Select KS3, then Maths. These are great resources to use at home or in the classroom.

Maths resources for home learning: secondary

www.stem.org.uk/home-learning/secondary-maths

These are resources to support secondary maths learning at home collated by STEM Learning. This is an extensive resource with a variety of maths games, activities and puzzles. Excellent.

STEM Learning: A Level maths

www.stem.org.uk/alevel-maths

This has extensive resources for A Level maths programmes of study covering Pure, Mechanics and Statistics. To access the resources, you are required to complete the free registration.

STEM Learning: secondary core maths

www.stem.org.uk/core-maths/resources

This has resources for GCSE higher-level topics. To access the resources, you are required to complete the free registration.

STEM Learning: secondary GCSE mathematics

www.stem.org.uk/secondary-maths

This has extensive resources covering KS3 and KS4 programmes of study. To access the resources, you are required to complete the free registration.

C MODERN FOREIGN LANGUAGES (MFL)

The resources below offer a range to practice language skills and a few that are specific to a topic or information that may add some variation to language learning. For language testing using worksheets, games and quizzes, a popular option is Quizlet (**www.quizlet.com** - select Languages, then either French, Spanish, German or Latin). Also have a look at Duolingo (**www.duolingo.com**), which has free language learning for different levels.

Learning resources and activities

Primary school teaching ideas

www.teachingideas.com/subjects/languages

This provides a large collection of downloadable display materials, resources and ideas for KS1 and KS2 language learning and practice. The resources cover Spanish, French, German and Sign Language. Despite being aimed at KS1 and KS2, these resources and activities would benefit KS3 pupils as a revision tool. Excellent resources to use in the classroom and at home.

Screening Languages

www.screeninglanguages.org

An online resource from the British Film Institute for MFL teachers and education practitioners to find research, information and examples of how short film can be used for languages in the classroom. With lesson plans and schemes of work this is an excellent resource.

French

Brand evolution: learning resource in French

www.museumofbrands.com/online-resources

A learning resource in French looking at brand design, which may be a useful exercise for French language learning pupils.

Children's University: French

www.childrensuniversity.manchester.ac.uk/learning-activities/languages

Introductory French language modules from the Children's University.

Dartmoor legends in French

www.dartmoor.gov.uk/enjoy-dartmoor/funzone/dartmoor-legends

All the Dartmoor legends are available in French, along with the English version. Just select French. Useful for French comprehension practice.

French Teacher

www.frenchteacher.net

This has a vast number of resources available. Select Free Stuff.

World War 1

www.bl.uk/teaching-resources/france-bnf-theme1

This teaching resource has been contributed by the Bibliothéque National de France and is designed to help teachers and students use World War 1 learning within the French history curriculum. This is also a good resource to use within the French language curriculum.

Zut!

www.zut.org.uk

This has interactive activities for French. Select either Beginner Year 7-9; Intermediate Year 10-11; or Advanced Year 12-13. If you use the site between 9am-4pm weekdays there is a subscription, but the rest of the time it is free.

German

Gut!

https://gut.languageskills.co.uk

This has interactive activities for German. Select either Beginner Year 7-9; Intermediate Year 10-11; or Advanced Year 12-13. If you use the site between 9am-4pm weekdays there is a subscription, but the rest of the time it is free.

Spanish

Español Extra

www.espanol-extra.co.uk

This has some free online Spanish resources for teachers and learners.

Oye!

https://oye.languageskills.co.uk

This has interactive activities for Spanish. Select either Beginner Year 7-9; Intermediate Year 10-11; or Advanced Year 12-13. If you use the site between 9am-4pm weekdays there is a subscription, but the rest of the time it is free.

The Vivarium

www.mmfromhome.com/resource-for-home-educators-and-fam

An environmental education activity with worksheets produced in English and Spanish from Manchester Museum. Scroll down to The Vivarium. The Spanish vocabulary describing animals and habitats makes this a useful resource for primary Spanish language learning. Suitable for KS1 and KS2.

MONEY

Understanding money and how finance, banks and economics work is part of the Personal, Social, Health and Economic Education (PSHE) and Citizenship curriculums for children and young people from all four nations. The aim is to prepare them for handling and managing their own money in the future and is often the element that PSHE study covers. The wider understanding of the synergy between the economy, money and banks is usually part of Citizenship. However, it does appear that this is not always the case. In order to make life a little less complicated, all of the resources have been collated together here. In addition, there are resources that look at the history and development of coinage, which for younger children can be a good starting point when talking about money.

Coins and notes

Ancient Greek coins

www.ashmolean.org/learning-resource-ancient-greece

Learning resource from the Ashmolean Museum. Select and download Coin Information for Teachers.

British Museum coins and banknotes activities

How do you construct a 50p?

www.britishmuseum.org/learn/schools/ages-11-14/classroom-resource-how-do-you-construct-50p

Which coin is which?

www.britishmuseum.org/learn/schools/ages-11-14/classroom-resource-which-coin-which

Note-ably different

www.britishmuseum.org/learn/schools/ages-11-14/classroom-resource-note-ably-different

These are three resources for KS3 geometry but are interesting coin-related tasks to tackle at home and for problem-solving.

Coins around the world

www.royalmint.com/the-royal-mint-experience/explore-the-exhibition/coins-around-the-world

The coins produced by the Royal Mint, for the United Kingdom and for many countries around the world, offer insights into history.

Coins through the ages

www.salisburymuseum.org.uk/learning/family-learning

Select Coins Through the Ages from Resources for Families at Home for a short downloadable resource to learn about different types of coins and how to make your own currency using everyday materials.

Currency converter 1270–2017

www.nationalarchives.gov.uk/currency-converter

Calculate purchasing power and find out how many animals, stores of wool and quarters of wheat you could buy and how much you could earn. Absolutely fascinating and great for projects.

Decimalisation

www.co-operativeheritage.coop/homeschooling-resources

An interesting, well-presented resource for children to convert shop prices from old money to the 1971 decimalisation. Children will learn what things cost 50 years ago and do some maths exercises to convert prices. Select Co-op Conversion Maths Exercise.

Ely Museum: coins

www.elymuseum.org.uk/uncategorised/museumfromhome-coins

This is a downloadable resource looking at the development of coinage.

How money started

https://ancienthistory.mrdonn.org/money.html

This provides an overview of the development of money and the introduction of coins.

Money

www.bankofengland.co.uk/education/home-learning-hub

Select Pounds & Pence for a series of films from the Bank of England on the history of money, why prices change and banknote security.

Money during World War 2

www.tankmuseum.org/wp-content/uploads/2020/04/Old-Money-Maths-KS2.pdf

An old money maths activity from the Tank Museum.

Money fun

www.bankofengland.co.uk/education/home-learning-hub

Select Family Fun for activities to enjoy together. This has excellent resources to design your own money, banknote word searches and a banknote checker game.

Royal Mint: learning resources

www.royalmint.com/kids

From tooth fairies to Paddington and covering Geography, History, Science and Literacy - and not forgetting coin collecting - the Activities for Kids educational tools from the Royal Mint are well worth exploring. Excellent.

Economics

Economics for 16–18-year-olds

www.bankofengland.co.uk/education/home-learning-hub/post-16-economics-learning-resources

Aimed at 16-18-year-olds, but equally useful to parents and teachers, these resources help young people to understand what the Bank of England does, Monetary Policy and Financial Stability.

Economics for young people (EconoME)

www.nationalschoolspartnership.com/iniatives/econome

These are resources from the Bank of England via the national school's partnership. They are an excellent set of resources for 11-16-year-olds that inform young people about economics, finance and their money decision-making. It has structured lessons plans. It requires signing up to the national school's partnership, which teachers and parents can do to receive all free resources and lesson plans.

The economy made simple

www.bankofengland.co.uk/knowledgebank

A fantastic set of fact pages covering What is Money?; What do banks do?; What is the economy?; What are interest rates?; What is GDP?; What is inflation?; What is insurance?; Who sets exchange rates?; and What does the bank of England do?. All aimed at children from 11 years old and for use by teachers as a learning resource. There are many more pages to select from the three Knowledge Banks - Money, Payments and Spending; Banks, Borrowing and Saving; and Learn about the Economy.

Money management

Bank of England home learning

www.bankofengland.co.uk/education/home-learning-hub

Packed with information for class and home use. Excellent.

Lloyds Bank Academy: empower young people with financial skills

www.lloydsbankacademy.co.uk/financial-skills

This provides session packs from Lloyds Bank Academy to help improve the financial capability skills of young people. Each is designed to suit the target age-group and has resources that can be used one-to-one or with a group. Excellent.

Mon£y Marvel$

www.museumonthemound.com/schools/mon£y-marvel

Money Marvels is a series of short videos to support the teaching of money as a topic. The resource is from the Museum on the Mound, Edinburgh. This links to

Beads, Bawbees and Banknotes, an interdisciplinary resource for teachers. Access to the resources requires teachers in Scotland to register for free. It covers What is Money? History of Coinage; Banknotes; and Keeping Money Safe. Suitable for P5-P7 or could be adapted for younger children.

My Money Week resource hub

www.young-enterprise.org.uk/MMW

My Money Week is a national activity for primary and secondary children and young people providing and helping them to gain skills in money management. Both parents/carers and teachers can register for access to free downloadable resources, including Home Learning Guides and lesson plans for KS1, KS2, KS3 and KS4 (including those from previous years back to 2014). This is a fantastic resource for an important life skill. Excellent.

MUSIC

Music is a vast subject area with many varied levels and forms of study. Most children will experience some music learning during their time at school, with some progressing to study GCSE and A Level or the equivalent. Some children will learn to play an instrument either at school or from home. And most children and young people grow up listening to and developing their own music preferences.

The resources here reflect music learning at school and informal music learning at home. There are a host of resources from some fantastic organisations such as the Royal College of Music and the Royal Opera House. There is also information included on Instruments; Composers; Music Teachers; and Types of Music. In addition, have a look at **www.music-education.co.uk** which has a vast array of music resources for primary and home schooling.

Information

All the musical instruments of the world

www.allthemusicalinstrumentsoftheworld.com

Musical instruments shown in A-Z order with a colour picture. It offers the option to view an image of all the instruments being played or to view all the instruments by classification. A gem of a resource.

Lyrics A–Z

www.azlyrics.com

Search by the artist/band name or song title for full lyrics of hundreds of songs. Fantastic.

Learning resources and activities

British Library: teaching resources: music

www.bl.uk/teaching-resources?teachingsubjects=music

This has downloadable teaching resources from the British Library for A Level music students. They are linked to online resources.

GCSE music resource pack

www.beatlesstory.com/teacher-resources

This resource pack focuses on GCSE music in accordance with the AQA specification. It supports teachers, parents and pupils in their exploration of the Beatles' Sgt Pepper's Lonely Hearts Club Band. Scroll though the list of resources and select GCSE Music Resource Pack.

Music resources

www.musicteachers.co.uk/resources

This has downloadable classroom and teaching materials for children and young people. Select resources for Ages 4+; Ages 14+; or Ages 16+. Relevant topics are covered with age groups and include Understanding Simple Rhythmic Notation through to Composition and Musicology and many more. There is also a General section that includes aural tests by grades along with downloadable manuscript paper templates. It has an excellent E-Zone, which has extensive music theory HD Video Tutorials and downloadable PDF worksheets. It includes a Glossary of Musical Terms, along with interactive Aural Training with tracking scores, pitch recognition, hundreds of musical examples and high-quality audio recordings. Excellent.

Primary school teaching ideas

www.teachingideas.co.uk/subjects/music

This offers KS1 and KS2 downloadable teaching resources. The resources, ideas and activities include Music Composition; Instruments; Musical Elements; and Notation. It also has templates to print Manuscript Paper with either 6 or 10 staves.

Royal College of Music: learning resources

www.rcm.ac.uk/sparks/digitalresources

The Royal College of Music has produced digital resources for use in school or at home. The majority are aimed at 5-11-year-olds. They are very well produced with an activity pack and accompanying recorded or printed sheet music resources for each topic.

Royal Opera House: learning resources

https://learning-platform.roh.org.uk

The Royal Opera House Learning Platform has cross-curricular creative learning activities for children and young people linked to the National Curriculum for Dance, Music and Art & Design. The content of the learning platform has been written by teachers offering a wonderful set of creative education resources for teachers, educators and young people from KS1 onwards. In addition, it provides a set of lesson plans on opera and dramatic singing aimed primarily at younger children up to 11 years. There are also some simple activities to do at home. Select Create & Learn.

Composers

Classical composers index

www.music-scores.com/composer.php

A simple list of composers organised alphabetically by surname with the year born, the year died and nationality.

Composer index

www.boosey.com

Excellent composer index from Boosey & Hawkes - the classical music publisher. It also includes the Boosey & Hawkes photographic resource spanning the past 100 years and includes composers, operas and dance.

Gustav Holst – The Planets Project

www.lpo.org.uk/creative-classrooms-connect/holst-s-the-planets-for-key-stage-2.html

This resource is designed to be used in the classroom but could equally be used at home. It aims to equip children to enjoy and understand more about the London Philharmonic Orchestra and to find out more about Holst's *The Planets*. The structure of this learning resource is excellent and will enliven any music lesson.

Hinduism and Holst

www.holstmuseum.org.uk/learning

A short downloadable resource exploring the composer Holst and his interest in India and Hinduism. This offers an interesting starting point to further exploration. There is also a SEN resource. Select Hinduism and Holst or Hinduism and Holst SEN.

Opera composers

www.eno.org/discover-opera/composers

A very useful and detailed guide from English National Opera on opera composers, including biographical details, musical style and notable works.

The Gracious Muse: Benjamin Britten and Peter Pears

www.museumcrush.org/the-gracious-muse-benjamin-britten-and-peter-pears

Find out about the inspiration Benjamin Britten took from his partner, Peter Pears.

Composition and theory

Composition: learning from Delius and Elgar

www.bl.uk/teaching-resources/20th-century-music-composition

A downloadable teaching pack from the British Library for A Level students. The pack suggests reading and digitised materials that students can access and provides a range of activities enabling them to use Delius' and Elgar's music to develop their own compositional skills. Excellent.

Music theory

www.musictheory.net

This provides music lessons covering music basics; rhythm and meter; scales and key signatures; intervals; chords; diatonic chords; chord progressions; and

Neapolitan chords. It also has exercises and tools available online for free. A good starting point for working on music theory and for practice exercises.

Sheet music: orchestras, recorders and brass ensembles

www.musicbyarrangement.co.uk

Select Free Stuff for free downloadable sheet music for Easy Orchestra; Easy Recorders; and Easy Brass Ensemble. It is aimed at school bands and music groups but equally useful for home practice.

Sheet music: violin and viola

www.violinandviola.co.uk

This provides free sheet music available as Adobe PDF documents. It covers a wide range, including Chamber Music; Duets; String Orchestra; and Solos. It also has downloadable teaching resources, including manuscript paper. Excellent.

Music festivals

The history of Glastonbury Festival

www.vam.ac.uk/articles/the-history-of-glastonbury-festival

Fashioning Glastonbury Festival

www.vam.ac.uk/articles/fashioning-glastonbury-festival

Glastonbury Festival stage design

www.vam.ac.uk/articles/glastonbury-festival-stage-design

These are three excellent articles from the Victoria and Albert Museum, the guardian since 2014 of the Glastonbury Festival Archive. For KS3 and KS4 students looking for project material this is a great resource.

Music teachers

Music teachers

www.musicteachers.co.uk

Find a local music teacher for your chosen instrument and level of experience.

Opera

A brief history of opera

www.operanorth.co.uk/explore-opera/a-brief-history-of-opera

Discover how opera came into being with this potted history from Opera North.

English National Opera

www.eno.org/discover-opera

Select Discover Opera to explore a wealth of information on the English National

Opera's past and present productions. A synopsis is given of each opera performed, plus images and films.

Opera North: A–Z guide to opera

www.operanorth.co.uk/explore-opera/a-z-of-opera

An A-Z guide to all things opera. It includes images and sound.

Welsh National Opera: family activities

www.wno.org.uk/family-activities

A lovely set of family activities that are fun and engaging to share and all available to print. It includes an opera-themed word search and templates to make opera props. These include a bat mask for the masked ball in *Die Fledermaus* by Johann Strauss II and a headdress from *Carmen* by Georges Bizet, along with many more. A great way to introduce opera to younger children and families. Excellent.

Orchestra

Royal Albert Hall: family learning resources

www.royalalberthall.com/about-the-hall/education/content-for-families-during-lockdown

Select Meet the Orchestra for musicians to introduce the instruments in the orchestra. Download the fabulous booklet *My Great Orchestra Adventure* for an introduction to each instrument - this is an excellent, clear and colourful booklet that should be available in every school. In addition, there are related colouring sheets.

The Young Person's Guide to the Orchestra

www.rpo.co.uk/rpo-at-home/young-person-s-guide

A great way to introduce the orchestra to children and young people, created by the Royal Philharmonic Orchestra.

Popular music

The Beatles Story: learning resources

www.beatlesstory.com/teacher-resources

This has a KS1 and KS2 Resource Pack that gives an overview of the history of The Beatles. There are also a host of online educational activities to download linked to song writing, album cover art, create an instrument and music that influenced The Beatles. It gives lots of ideas for popular music topics. This could also be useful for KS3.

Mods, rockers, skinheads, punks: snapshots of Southend's subcultural history

www.museumcrush.org/mods-rockers-skinheads-punks-snapshots-of-southends-subcultural-history

This offers a look at the social history of the 1960s and 1970s music scenes. The archive photographs are interesting when considering popular culture and the role of fashion within music.

Reggae music

www.museumcrush.org/exploring-londons-dub-reggae-roots
Find out about the impact, Dub (the use of the recording studio itself as an instrument) has had on the music industry.

Traditional music

Ceòl nan Gàidheal

www.nls.uk/learning-zone/creativity
This dual Gaelic/English learning resource provides an overview of historic sources, songs, instruments and the Living Tradition of Gaelic Music.

Using music for educational needs

Coastline for 3–5-year-olds

www.aberdeencity.gov.uk/AAGM/learn/families/early-years-3-5yrs
Using the painting *A Ground Swell, Carradale* by William McTaggart and the sound of waves and traditional rhymes to think about the sea, this resource is designed to encourage younger children to respond to the pieces through movement. A very thoughtful resource from Aberdeen Archives, Gallery & Museums that could be used as a template for other themes using art and music.

Florence Nightingale Museum: Florence Nightingale and mental health

www.florence-nightingale.co.uk/free-learning-resources
This is an activity for KS1 and KS2 looking at how music changes how people feel. It is a simple activity to do at school or at home and allows children to think about how feelings can be affected.

Music and dyslexia

www.bdadyslexia.org.uk/advice/children
Select Music and dyslexia for information on the needs of the dyslexic child studying music.

Using music to understand maths

www.royalalberthall.com/about-the-hall/education/content-for-families-during-lockdown
Select Discover Music & Maths. Discover the link between maths and music with the help of tuba playing from the Royal Albert Hall. The sessions link to the KS2 curriculum using music to help understand some basic mathematical principles

and how maths can be used to create a piece of music. Great for use at home or in the classroom.

Using music to understand science

www.royalalberthall.com/about-the-hall/education/content-for-families-during-lockdown
Select Discover Music & Science. Links to the KS3 curriculum to use music to gain a greater understanding of key scientific principles.

MYTHS AND LEGENDS

See also: Famous and inspirational people

Myths and legends have been part of world storytelling for hundreds of years. Many myths and legends are important elements of the heritage and cultural history of a country. As a learning tool, the use of stories from Greek Mythology or British Folklore or Afro-Caribbean Tales, to name but a few, can inspire and develop creative writing, drama and literacy skills. Some lesser-known myths from around the world are also included below.

Information

Encyclopedia Mythica

www.pantheon.org/mythology

Packed with information on mythology from across the world and from ancient civilisations. It includes folklore covering the Arthurian Legends, British Folklore and General Folklore.

England's myths and legends

www.visitbritain.com/gb/en/englands-most-spine-tingling-myths-and-legends

A short list of myths and legends attributed to areas of England. A good starting point for projects on English folk tales, specifically legends.

Greek mythology

www.mythweb.com

This provides definitions of the main gods and heroes of Greek mythology using images and cartoon characters.

Myths and legends

www.history-for-kids.com/myths-and-legends.html

The stories from myths and legends are presented here as short story poems. Not only are they great fun but offer an easy alternative to learning about the characters and tales. Well worth a visit.

Myths and legends coursework guide

www.tate.org.uk/art/student-resource/exam-help/myths-and-legends

Using art, the Tate Gallery has produced an excellent resource to inspire work around myths and legends. Not only is the resource excellent for KS3 students, it is also useful for teachers as inspiration and ideas for the topic of myths and legends with young children.

Mythstories

www.mythstories.com
Select Educational Resources for an eclectic mix of myths and folk stories. There are some resources available in French and Welsh.

Learning resources and activities

Greek myths

https://greece.mrdonn.org
Greek myths retold for children. Select Teachers for a host of related class and home activities.

Greek mythology: primary resource

www.natgeokids.com/uk/primary-resource/greek-mythology-primary-resource
Learn about the gods, goddesses, monsters and heroes of Ancient Greece.

Myths and legends project plans

www.teachingtimes.com/mythsandlegendsliteracyprojectplans
This is available on open access to download. It offers a wealth of ideas exploring the myths and legends and related story writing. This could be adapted for class or home use and includes colour images. Excellent.

Myths and legends teaching pack

www.teachingideas.co.uk/writing-fiction/the-myths-and-legends-pack
This free downloadable pack may not be the best graphically but is packed with information that could be used for learning either at home or at school.

Specific myths

Australian Aboriginal inspired stories: a literacy resource for teachers and parents

www.dormanmuseum.co.uk/learning/australian-aboriginal-inspired-stories
A great resource with video clips of Aboriginal stories such as 'How Kangaroo got her pouch'. Includes downloadable instructions on creating stories inspired by the Aboriginal myths. Excellent.

Dartmoor legends

www.dartmoor.gov.uk/enjoy-dartmoor/funzone/dartmoor-legends
Who of us realised there were quite so many Dartmoor legends?!

The myth of the Kelpies

www.culturestreet.org.uk/lessons.php
Select the Myth of the Kelpies. This provides a lesson plan to explore the Scottish

myth and Gaelic folklore of the Kelpies through art and writing. Not only does the lesson plan provide interesting ideas and structure but also lends itself to a model for exploring other myths, legends and folklore.

Snowdonian myths and legends

www.visitsnowdonia.info/myths-and-legends

The myths and legends of the Snowdonia Mountains.

The Story of Anansi and his Sons: an audiobook and lesson plan

http://schools.fairtrade.org.uk/resource/the-story-of-anansi-and-his-sons-an-audiobook-and-lesson-plan

The story of Anansi and his Sons is a traditional West African folk story that can be enjoyed at home or in the classroom. It is suitable for children from 7 - 14 years. The accompanying teaching notes include a guide for interactive storytelling, a group activity and prompts for discussion.

The Welsh dragon and the Welsh flag

www.visitwales.com/info/history-heritage-and-traditions/dragon-spirit-legend-welsh-dragon

Find out about the legend of the Welsh dragon.

NATURE

Enjoying nature and wildlife provides lots of learning opportunities for all. Here are a variety of resources for children, young people and families from a range of museums and organisations, including the National Trust, Forestry England and the RSPB, to name a few. Learning doesn't get more enjoyable than this!

Information

iSpot

www.ispotnature.org

Great for wildlife identification and created by the Open University.

Oxford University Museum of Natural History: learning zone

www.oum.ox.ac.uk/thezone

Designed for younger children to find facts and information on insects.

UK Safari

www.uksafari.com

This has an extensive Identify It facility covering an A–Z of wildlife from Amphibians to Wild Flowers, all with colour photos.

Learning resources and activities

Canal & River Trust: learning resources

www.canalrivertrust.org.uk/explorers/resources

This is an excellent learning resource with a wealth of downloadable wildlife explorer trails within the list of resources. Using the filter select either Animals, Habitats or the Environment. Excellent.

Centre of Alternative Technology: wildlife activities

www.cat.org.uk/cat-at-home/cat_at_home-families

A great selection of wildlife activities including the downloadable Winter Wildlife activity booklet.

Connecting to nature

www.chatsworth.org/your-visit/learning/learning-resources/resources-for-ages-5-7

A learning resource aimed at KS1 and KS2 from Chatsworth House. It explores the use of our senses to connect with nature and to discover ways that animals adapt to survive. Select Connecting to Nature. Excellent.

Dartmoor National Park

www.dartmoor.gov.uk/enjoy-dartmoor/funzone/games

This has nature activities to do at home or in the classroom.

Dens and shelters

www.chatsworth.org/your-visit/learning/learning-resources/resources-for-ages-5-7

Learn how to build dens and shelters outside or in your home with Chatsworth House. This activity also looks at why shelters are important for animals and how they might build them. It is aimed at KS1 and KS2. Select Dens and Shelters.

Dorset County Museum: natural activities

www.dorsetcountymuseum.org/learn

Select from the Natural Dorset Activities list for things to do while out and about. It includes a Wildflower Spotter Guide.

Durham Cathedral: make a sound card

www.durhamcathedral.co.uk/learning/online-resources

Select Get Creative at Home for downloadable instructions on making a sound card to record the sounds we hear when we stop and listen. Great for in the garden or on a nature walk.

Forests at home

www.forestryengland.uk/forests-at-home

A great set of nature activities for all the family. Requires registering for free downloadable activities.

The Garden Museum: family activity sheets

www.gardenmuseum.org.uk/learning/children-and-families

This has downloadable sheets on How to Press Your Own Flowers and Make a Wildlife Collage, plus an excellent information sheet on Bees.

Jodrell Bank: garden activities

www.jodrellbank.net/garden-activities

Downloadable activities to enjoy outdoors.

Museum of Zoology: nature classroom

www.museumofzoologyblog.com/category/nature-classroom

Extensive activities and information to explore nature, looking at animals, plants and wildlife. Select Nature Classroom.

National Trust: things to do

www.nationaltrust.org.uk/things-to-do

This has activities for families to enjoy outdoors. Select 50 Things to do Before You're 11¾. It has lots of outdoor activities to do all year round and a downloadable chart to complete. A really inspiring activity list for children and their families or for schools to enjoy.

Natural History Museum: exploring nature

www.nhm.ac.uk/take-part/try-this-at-home.html

This is packed with activities to do at home for looking at, exploring and spotting nature. There are some particular items worth mentioning (although all the resources are brilliant): the UK Tree interactive Identification Guide and the UK Bumblebee ID Guide. Excellent.

The Natural World: children's activity pack

www.derbymuseumsfromhome.com/explore-and-discover

Inspired by the animals in the collection at Derby Museums, the downloadable pack for children is packed with activities to explore and discover the natural world. It would be great to use at home and for classroom ideas. Suitable for 5-11 years old. Select The Natural World: Children's Activity Pack.

Pembrokeshire Coast wildlife

www.pembrokeshirecoast.wales/about-the-national-park/wildlife

This has a selection of downloadable wildlife leaflets for along the Pembrokeshire Coast.

Portsmouth Natural History: nature activity sheets

www.portsmouthnaturalhistory.co.uk/get-involved/activities

A collection of downloadable nature-related activity sheets from Cumberland House Natural History Museum.

Royal Society for the Protection of Birds: fun and learning

www.rspb.org.uk/fun-and-learning

This has loads of ideas and resources for children and their families to connect with nature using simple activities to do at home and at school that explore wildlife. It also has downloadable activity sheets for educators covering Homes for Nature; Wildlife Detective; Food & Water for Nature; and Spotting Nature. Excellent.

Seasonal nature walks

www.greatnorthmuseum.org.uk/learning/museum-activities-from-home-or-school

This has downloadable nature walks for Summer, Autumn and Winter with links to other online sources for plant and animal identification. Select Summer Nature Walk, Autumn Nature Walk, Winter Nature Walk or Urban Nature Walk.

Spot it sheets

www.rspb.org.uk/fun-and-learning/for-teachers/lesson-plans-and-supporting-resources/spot-it

The Spot it downloadable sheets cover minibeasts; birds and mammals; flowering plants; tracks and signs; nuts and berries; trees and shrubs; and ponds. They are colourful identifying sheets that would be great to use at school, on class visits, at home or on family day trips.

Take notice of nature cards

www.derbymuseumsfromhome.com/explore-and-discover

A wonderful and downloadable resource from Derby Museums using five cards with activities to do either in the garden or at the park. The cards include: Take notice of nature; Be active in nature; Keep learning about nature; Connect with people through nature; and Give back to nature. Select the Natural World, then Take Notice of Nature Cards. Excellent.

The Wildlife Trusts: help wildlife at home

www.wildlifetrusts.org/actions

This has loads of simple activities that children, young people and their families can do to help wildlife. The activities range from how to build a hedgehog home to how to provide water for wildlife. A great learning tool, which can be adapted for use in the classroom.

Wetland and Wildlife Trust

www.wwt.org.uk/discover-wetlands

Within Explore Wetlands, select Home Learning and Family Fun for learning sessions developed by the learning team that cover Wetland Wildlife; Food Chains; Migration; Lifecycles; Trees; and Minibeasts, along with many more. For each there is a home learning session plan for either 5-7-year-olds or 7-11-year-olds with a related activity to make. Excellent.

Woodland Trust: activities for nature-loving kids

www.woodlandtrust.org.uk/blog/2020/03/nature-detectives

This has simple, nature-based activities to do at home, in the garden or at the local wood.

Gardening

Gardening fun

www.rhs.org.uk/education-learning/gardening-children-schools/family-activities

This gives some simple outdoor activities for families to enjoy together, offering learning opportunities while having outdoor fun.

RHS Campaign for School Gardening

https://schoolgardening.rhs.org.uk/resources

This is packed with resources, activities, information sheets, lesson plans and spotter guides, not only for teachers but for all educators and parents. It is exceptional in its coverage and inspiring for getting children and families outdoors, planting, growing and finding out about nature and the environment. Excellent.

Worm activities

www.museum.wales/cardiff/learning/resources

This includes a worm word search - you'll be surprised at how many different types of worms there are!

Insects

Buglife

www.buglife.org.uk/get-involved/children-and-schools

This is the Invertebrate Conservation Trust and is packed with information about bugs. It also has resources for children and schools. Select Activities for Schools for School Packs linked to the curriculum with downloadable lesson plans. Or select Activities to Do with Children for a host of fun things for children to do connected to bugs, which includes making a bee hotel or a mini-meadow. Excellent.

Butterfly conservation

www.butterfly-conservation.org

This has an A-Z of UK Butterflies, an A-Z of European Butterflies and an A-Z of Moths. Plus, there is an identify a butterfly or moth facility.

Make your own paper insect collection

www.cowleyroadworks.org

A great resource developed in partnership between Cowley Road Works and Oxford University to learn about the environment and insects. It has videos about insects from the University of Oxford's Museum of Natural History, with downloadable resources for parents and teachers including printable templates of insects, labels and worksheets. Select Make It, then Learning Projects. It also includes a Bee Hotel too.

Minibeasts

www.museumsandgalleries.leeds.gov.uk/virtual-visit/online-activities/activities-for-kids

Select Minibeast activities for a host of videos and downloadable activity sheets.

Munching Caterpillars

www.munchingcaterpillars.org

This is a campaign for children from the Butterfly Conservation. It is packed with downloadable resources for teachers and families from identifying butterflies and moths and their caterpillars to life cycles and creating butterfly gardens.

Pollination

www.chatsworth.org/your-visit/learning/learning-resources/resources-for-ages-5-7
A downloadable resource from Chatsworth House to learn about pollination and how it contributes to the life cycle of plants. Aimed at KS1 and KS2. Select Pollination.

Seaside

Marine wildlife

www.wildlifetrusts.org/wildlife-explorer/marine
Discover marine species with the Wildlife Trusts, complete with colour photos and information.

Rockpool explorer's checklist

www.titanicbelfast.com/learningresources.aspx
Select Rockpool Explorer's Checklist for a printable fun factsheet.

Trees and plants

Plant and fungal science: learning resources

www.kew.org/learning/learning-at-home
Kew Gardens has a series of resources about plant and fungal science, all curriculum aligned for KS1 to KS5. They are downloadable and include videos, games and challenges. It also has an online learning platform called Endeavor, which has teaching resources for KS1 to KS5. This has videos, infographics and whiteboard presentations all free to use by registering your school to access the resource at **www.kew.org/learning/endeavour**

Tree ID for kids

www.woodlandtrust.org.uk/blog/2020/03/tree-id-kids
This has downloadable and printable tree ID guides for children to learn about trees either at home in the garden, at school in the playground or in a local wood. It has Leaf ID; Twig ID; Blossom & catkin ID: and Fruit, Nut & Seed ID.

Trees, woods and wildlife

www.woodlandtrust.org.uk
The Woodland Trust provides a wealth of information, including the A–Z of British Trees, Ancient Trees, how trees fight climate change and flooding, through to the animals and birds that trees and woods support. There are learning resources for schools too: select Support Us, then Your School, to find out about Tree Tools for Schools.

OLYMPICS

Since the birth in 1896 of the first modern Olympic Games, children and young people have been fascinated, inspired and motivated by this spectacle of sporting ability from world athletes. Find out more about the history and the participants from the resources below. The Olympics theme can also be incorporated into other learning with some ideas given below. There are also lots of facts and figures about the Olympics and Olympic records in the Guinness World Records (**www.guinnessworldrecords.com**).

Information

Do you know the Olympic Games?

www.olympic.org/museum/visit/schools/teaching-resources/support-de-cours/how-well-do-you-know-the-olympic-games

This provides an introduction to the Olympic movement and the Olympic Games. Lots of information interspersed with colourful cartoon pictures.

Olympics

www.olympic.org

This provides a list and details of all Olympic Games, Olympic Winter Games and Olympic Youth Games. Provides information about the Olympic Torch and Olympic medals, all with images and a wealth of athlete information, including photographs from past Olympics.

Olympic posters

www.olympic.org/museum/visit/schools/teaching-resources/support-de-cours/olympic-posters

Learning resources and activities

The Olympic Games in Ancient Greece

www.britishmuseum.org/learn/schools

The British Museum has downloadable resources by key stages. For Ancient Greece, select Key Stage 2 to access a resource document on the Olympic Games.

The Olympic Games in Antiquity

www.olympic.org/museum/visit/schools/teaching-resources/support-de-cours/the-olympic-games-in-antiquity

Fantastic learning resource looking at the Olympic Games.

The Olympic Museum

www.olympic.org/museum/visit/schools/teaching-resources

There are a wide range of teaching materials available from the Olympic Museum arranged by theme. They cover Creative & Manual Activities; Human and Social Services; Information Communications Technology; Mathematical and Natural Sciences.

Also try **www.teachingideas.co.uk/pe/the-olympic-museum-resources** to access resources from the Olympic Museum. Excellent.

Ways to use the Olympics in the Classroom

www.teachingideas.co.uk/athletics/ways-to-use-the-olympics-in-the-classroom
A brilliant list of ideas and suggestions of how to use the Olympics for classroom or home learning for English; Maths; Science; Computing; Design & Technology; Art; Music; Geography; History; Language; and PE. Excellent.

OUT AND ABOUT

See also: Nature

Getting out and about offers lots of learning opportunities. This section covers getting out using pedal and pedestrian power, both of which are great for seeing nature and wildlife, while not forgetting visits to your local museum or library. Have a look out for the Heritage Open Days (**www.heritageopendays.org.uk**) during September each year, when hundreds of hidden places are open to the public - discover, learn and have fun.

Cycling and walking

Bikeability

www.bikeability.org.uk

Great resource for cycling, including family cycling and cycling to school.

Bikeability: just for fun

www.bikeability.org.uk/cycle-more/family-cycling/just-for-fun

Not quite outdoors but some fun family activities to do related to cycling.

British Cycling: cycling activities for kids and young people

www.britishcycling.org.uk/young-people

Canal & River explorers

www.canalrivertrust.org.uk/explorers/resources

This has a wealth of downloadable resources (175 individual topics in fact!) looking at: Canals; Waterways; Rivers; Birds; Locks; Aqueducts; and every named lock and aqueduct in England and Wales. Many of the resources have been linked to the curriculum covering History; Geography; Citizenship; and Science. It includes a filter facility for searching. Some resources are available in Welsh.

Cycling Scotland: nursery and schools resources

www.cycling.scot/resources/nursery-school

This has a wealth of resources for schools, parents/carers and children. It has a useful booklet called *Cycling Games*, which gives instructions for cycling activities. It is a must for developing confident cyclists and great fun too. Excellent.

HSBC UK Ready Set Ride

www.readysetride.co.uk

Quick and easy games to teach children to pedal created by HSBC UK British Cycling.

Let's Ride Local

www.letsridelocal.co.uk

HSBC UK Let's Ride Local provides ideas and inspiration to encourage family rides in local areas as well as hundreds of route listings. Find a route by searching by a chosen area.

Living Streets: learning resources

www.livingstreets.org.uk

Living Streets is the UK charity for walking and supports schools, families and communities to encourage walking every day. There are resources and documents to support walking initiatives for primary and secondary schools as well as parents, which includes the Family Walk to School kit.

Sustran cycling

www.sustrans.org.uk

This provides information on the National Cycle Network, the UK-wide network of signed paths and routes for walking, cycling, wheeling and exploring outdoors. It also has education activities to help increase physical activity.

Walking from home activity booklet for families

www.livingstreets.org.uk/walk-to-school/primary-schools

The *Walking from Home* activity booklet for families has 14 sets of activities suitable for families with primary age children. The resource sheets provide educational walking activities to support learning while staying active.

Destinations

Glasgow Museums: away for the day

www.glasgowlife.org.uk/museums/away-for-the-day

This had to be included! A fabulous booklet from Glasgow Museums designed for families to enjoy days out at their nine museums. Available in Arabic, Mandarin, Polish, Punjabi, Romanian and Urdu, as well as English. Top marks to Glasgow for the most family-friendly and well-designed booklet encouraging simple, free days out together.

Transport

National Motor Museum: activities

www.nationalmotormuseum.org.uk/learning/creative-activities

A collection of creative activities to engage and inspire children with the story of motoring.

C PE (PHYSICAL EDUCATION)

Most children will have PE at school as part of the curriculum, starting from Early Years until Year 11. Outside of school, many children will be involved in a sport or some form of physical exercise although not all share the same enthusiasm! There are a number of activities given below to get children and families active. Many organisations have produced resources that can be used at home. In addition, there are resources for students and teachers devising PE lesson plans and these too could be used at home. There are also some resources for PE activities with children with special educational needs or who need extra help through disability.

Information

NHS: sports and activities A–Z

www.nhs.uk/change4life/activities/sports-and-activities

This gives a definition of each sport and a link to find out more.

Learning resources and activities

Physical literacy

www.sport.wales/content-vault/physical-literacy

Excellent explanation of what physical literacy means by Sport Wales. This is a really useful resource for all PE students.

Primary school teaching ideas

www.teachingideas.co.uk/subjects/pe

A large collection of ideas and downloadable resources for KS1 and KS2 PE that can be used in the classroom or at home.

Sport England

www.sportengland.org/know-your-audience/demographic-knowledge/children-and-young-people

This has some great resources for PE students to consider as part of their studies.

Youth Sport Trust: PE activities

www.youthsporttrust.org/free-resources

This is packed with activities to do at school or at home and provides a wealth of activity ideas across PE units. It includes SEND activities and a host of family activities to keep everyone active. Excellent.

Youth Sports Trust: stay active staycation

www.youthsporttrust.org/family-hub

Select Stay Active. A great set of activities to keep children and young people active.

It includes Active Board Games; Garden Games; Indoor Activities; 60 Second Challenges; and an excellent resource for young people with profound or multiple learning difficulties based on the National Curriculum PE programme of study. Excellent.

Get active with individual sports

10 minute shake up games

www.nhs.uk/10-minute-shake-up/shake-ups

Fun activities to get the whole family moving either in or outdoors. Change4Life and Disney have teamed up to create play-along games inspired by Disney and Pixar characters. They are designed for 10-minute bursts of movement towards the 60 active minutes a day children need to keep healthy. Excellent.

Ballet: French impressions – 3–5-year-olds

www.aberdeencity.gov.uk/AAGM/learn/families/early-years-3-5yrs

This is a great resource from Aberdeen Art Gallery. It uses the sculpture of 'Balancing Ballet Dancer' by Degas to explore movement. It has a video clip of Matthew Bourne's *Swan Lake* and an audio clip of *The Swan* from the *Carnival of the Animals* by Saint-Saëns with movement activities for children to use to respond to the pieces. A very original and thoughtful resource that introduces children to art, music and movement. Select French Impressions (3-5yrs). An excellent template for developing further resources using other art pieces and music for a wider age range.

British Gymnastics: #GymnastsAtHome learning resources

www.british-gymnastics.org/news-and-events/news/latest-news/9033-gymnastsathome

Gymnastic related word searches and colouring sheets.

Cycling: Bikeability

www.bikeability.org.uk/tools-for-schools/learning-resources

This has learning resources that are curriculum-linked for EYFS, KS1 and KS2 and includes downloadable teacher guides and pupil resources. Excellent.

England Netball: Bee@Home

www.englandnetball.co.uk/bee-at-home

England Netball has a series of challenge videos for under 11s and families to help them keep active at home. In addition, there is a series of simple Bee@Home downloadable resources that includes a Bee Netball Target Board and Bee Netball Bingo, all linked to encouraging children to play netball but also great for just keeping active at home.

Football: family activities

www.nationalfootballmuseum.com/communities/stayathome

The National Football Museum's family friendly activities to do at home.

Football Association: coaching children 5–11 years

www.thefa.com/bootroom/resources/coaching

Fantastic for PE students faced with devising a coaching plan and equally valuable to teachers or parents developing children's football skills.

National Football Museum: football resources

www.padlet.com/nfmcommunities

This has learning sessions designed by and using the collections from the National Football Museum, covering a range of topics including Football and British Values; Football and Local History; Women; Football and Society; Leisure and Tourism; Early History of Football; and Football in the Modern World.

Royal Academy of Dance: children's online exercises

www.royalacademyofdance.org/rad-at-home/childrens-online-exercises

This has 12 ballet conditioning exercise videos for children at different levels as part of the RAD@Home.

Swim England: curriculum swimming and water safety resource packs

www.swimming.org/schools/resource-pack

This provides information for parents/carers, swimming teachers and primary schools. The guides are clear, structured and as such would be useful for those studying PE and looking at how swimming is taught and why and how it is delivered. It includes a great guide on water safety.

Specific topics

Coaching behaviours

www.ukcoaching.org/resources/topics/guides/coaching-behaviours

A useful resource for PE students looking at coaching from the participants' viewpoint and to consider coaching behaviours.

Cycling and my body

www.bikeabilit y.org.uk/tools-for-schools/learning-resources

Select KS1, then Cycling and My Body. This is a learning resource investigating how the heart works and the effects of cycling on the body. You can also select KS2 for My Heart - Beats Per Minute Tracking Fun.

Exercise

www.childrensuniversity.manchester.ac.uk/learning-activities/science/exercise/introduction

A great learning resource from the Children's University in Manchester and the Pharmacy Department at Manchester University as part of a *Healthy Living* project. It includes modules covering: Benefits of Exercise; Types of Exercise; The Muscles; Types of Muscles; The Heart; and The Pulse, with opportunities to test your knowledge throughout. This is perfect for PE students studying for GCSE or A Level.

Heart and circulation

www.abpischools.org.uk/topic/heartandcirculation/1/1

Excellent learning resource from the Association of the British Pharmaceutical Industry on the topic of the heart and circulation to support young people in understanding the subject.

NHS: indoor activities for kids

www.nhs.uk/change4life/activties/indoor-activities

Lots of indoor activities and games for children to keep them active.

Red, amber, green – roundabout

www.bikeability.org.uk/tools-for-schools/learning-resources

Select EYFS, then the Red, Amber, Green - Roundabout learning resource to develop gross motor and movement skills.

Sport and politics

www.economistfoundation.org/resources/#resources

Select Sport and Politics I or II for resources that explore, discuss, inform and analyse whether sport and politics should mix.

SEND children and PE

Disabled children in primary PE

www.disabilitysportwales.com/guidance-and-resources-for-primary-teachers

This gives guidance and resources for primary teachers from Disability Sport Wales. The resources are also useful for parents and carers.

Disabled children in secondary PE

www.disabilitysportwales.com/how-to-include-disabled-young-people-in-secondary-pe

This gives guidance and resources for secondary teachers from Disability Sport Wales. The resources are also useful for parents and carers.

NHS: accessible activities

www.nhs.uk/change4life/activities/accessible-activities

Activities for disabled children and young people to keep them active.

PE and dyspraxia

www.dyspraxiafoundation.org.uk/about-dyspraxia/information-sheets

Select from the list of information sheets 'Adjustments for PE for those with Dyspraxia/DCD' and 'PE Activities for Junior and Senior School Children who have Dyspraxia'. This gives downloadable information on delivering a PE lesson to a child with dyspraxia.

Sports and staying active for disabled people

www.activityalliance.org.uk/get-active/at-home

This is an excellent resource from the Activity Alliance: Disability Inclusion Sport on how disabled people can stay active at home or when going outside. It is packed with resources, exercise advice and activity guides that would be useful to PE students devising class programmes for children with disabilities or looking at the role of sport and health. They would equally be useful for considerations for any class group.

POPULATION

See also: Geography

There are lots of sources for population statistics, those listed below are some of the official sources used for the UK and the United Nations.

Information

Key figures on Europe

www.europa.eu/european-union/about-eu/figures

Select download Key Figures on Europe 2017. This is the latest edition available. In addition to statistics, it provides plenty of analysis and information.

Let's Count Census 2021

https://letscount.org.uk

The Office for National Statistics (ONS) provides a fantastic set of fourteen lesson plans covering the key areas of the English and Welsh curriculum. The lesson plans help to teach children about the importance of the census and how the information collected helps local areas. The lessons are accredited by Mathematics in Education and Industry (MEI), National Association for the Teaching of English (NATE) and the Geographical Association. The lessons cover: What is the census?; NHS and the census; Our school census; Equality, representation and the census; I count; Time travel detectives; Changing population; Working life in the past; Creating a time capsule; Lets count our local area; Planning for the future; and The year of the last census. It includes videos to use with the lesson plans and resources for children and parents. Excellent.

People, population and community

www.ons.gov.uk/peoplepopulationandcommunity

A wealth of UK statistics covering births, deaths and marriages, along with population and migration and health and social care amongst many others. This not only provides statistics but also commentary and analysis.

Population

www.un.org/en/sections/issues-depth/population/index.html

A wonderful resource looking at global population, providing statistics and discussion.

Population by country

www.worldpopulationreview.com/countries

This provides a ranked list of countries by 2020 population. It also gives the growth rate for 2019. In addition, you can see population by continents.

Population by world cities

www.worldpopulationreview.com/world-cities

This provides a list of world city populations ranked by 2020 population.

World Population Day

www.un.org/en/observances/world-population-day

Explores the issues around the global population and growth rate.

C PSHE (PERSONAL, SOCIAL, HEALTH AND ECONOMIC EDUCATION)

See also: Bullying; Citizenship; Change and loss; Drugs, alcohol and smoking; Health and wellbeing; Money; Relationships and sex

There is certainly a crossover with all the sections mentioned above. The resources included here are mainly those offering structured learning materials and tools directed specifically for PSHE teaching that is part of the National Curriculum. It is essential to use the other specific topics for further learning resources suitable for the individual elements of the PSHE programme of study.

Learning resources and activities

Childnet International: learning and teaching resources

www.childnet.com/resources/pshe-toolkit

A set of practical online safety PSHE toolkits to explore online issues with pupils aged 11 to 14 years, including links to relationships and sex and health education.

Primary school teaching ideas

www.teachingideas.co.uk/subjects/pshe

This has a large collection of Personal, Social, Health and Economic Education teaching ideas and resources for KS1 and KS2. It would also be useful with KS3 as a starting point for many discussions. Excellent for both classroom and home learning as well as for families to use together.

Social

All you need is love

www.beatlesstory.com/teacher-resources

Select Online Education Activity - PSHE (All You Need Is Love) to create a poster explaining how people can show love. Suitable for KS1 and KS2.

Organ and tissue donation

www.culturestreet.org.uk/teachers/organ_donation/lesson_plan.pdf

This lesson plan can be used with pupils to explore organ and tissue donation and the impact it has to save and improve lives. There is also an excellent True or False organ and tissue donation quiz produced by **www.organdonation.nhs.uk**, which is useful as a starting point to discuss the issue.

The Power of Kindness: learning resource

www.redcross.org.uk/get-involved/teaching-resources/kindness-calendar

Using the Power of Kindness calendar activity, children and young people can learn about and carry out kind acts. This resource from the British Red Cross includes a downloadable kindness calendar and supporting activities for 7 - 11-year-olds and 11 - 18-year-olds.

Tackling loneliness

www.redcross.org.uk/get-involved/teaching-resources/tackling-loneliness
This resource from the British Red Cross uses a range of mixed media resources to explore loneliness and how we can help people who feel lonely. Suitable for 7 - 18-year-olds. Excellent.

Health

P.E.riod Excuses by Jacqueline Wilson: let's talk about periods

www.wateraid.org/uk/get-involved/teaching/period-excuses-by-jacqueline-wilson
Imagine a free downloadable resource about periods called P.E.riod Excuses written especially by Jacqueline Wilson that is available as a short film and illustrated by Nick Sharratt and narrated by Jodie Whittaker! The film, short story and resources are fantastic.

Period Day

www.wateraid.org/uk/publications/period-day-in-school
28 May is Period Day. You'll find downloadable resources to discuss menstrual health and the issues for many girls around the world.

C RE (RELIGIOUS EDUCATION)

See also: Citizenship

Religion taught in UK schools looks at the six main world religions - Buddhism, Christianity, Hinduism, Islam, Judaism and Sikhism. Philosophy and Ethics are introduced and included for GCSE and A Level and some of the resources found in Citizenship will be useful for these.

Information

World faiths: RS for secondary schools

www.world-faiths.com

This is aimed at KS3 and KS4 and covers the six main world religions - Buddhism; Christianity; Hinduism; Islam; Judaism; and Sikhism. Also covers Philosophy and Ethics.

Learning resources and activities

British Library teaching resources: religious education

www.bl.uk/teaching-resources?curriculum=UK

Select Religious Education. A huge amount of teaching resources for religious education for 14-16 and 16-18-year-olds. Linked to the curriculum and covering Buddhism; Christianity; Hinduism; Islam; Judaism; Sikhism; and more. Includes further links to the British Library online resources. Excellent.

CAFOD (Catholic Agency for Overseas Development)

www.cafod.org.uk/Education/primary-teaching-resources

This has a wealth of lesson plans for the KS1 and KS2 RE curriculum. In addition, it has home learning resources for parents, children and schools for cross-curricular topics and RE project ideas and activities. It also provides assembly ideas for teachers on global themes and international days.

Durham Cathedral: worship resources for children

www.durhamcathedral.co.uk/learning/online-resources

Online resources for parents and carers to use at home with children. Linked to the liturgy used on Sunday and includes a related craft activity.

GCSE resources: RE

www.christianaid.org.uk/get-involved/schools/gcse-resources-re

GCSE lesson plan resources for RE written in conjunction with RE Today and Christian Aid.

World religions

www.teachingideas.co.uk/subjects/re

This has KS1 and KS2 downloadable teaching resources, ideas and activities. It includes Christianity; Islam; Judaism; Hinduism; and Sikhism. Excellent.

Buddhism

Buddha's birthday

www.dur.ac.uk/4schools/learningonline/familyactivities

This is an activity and brief explanation from the Oriental Museum to celebrate Buddha's birthday. It is a great activity to do at home or in the classroom. Select Buddha's Birthday.

Buddhism

www.thebuddhistsociety.org

To find out about aspects of Buddhism select Buddhism from the menu bar. For a list of books to use with children and young people, select Religious Education, then the Standing Advisory Councils on Religious Education (SACRE) Reading List.

Christianity

The rebuilding of a cathedral

www.stpauls.co.uk/learning-faith/schools-families/distance-learning

A great set of learning resources for looking at the topic of Places of Worship.

Sacred space

www.stpauls.co.uk/learning-faith/schools-families/distance-learning

Select Sacred Space to find out about St Paul's Patron Saints and Pentecost. In addition, there are some colouring sheets to download covering: Hope; Light; Love; and Peace.

The story of St Cuthbert – KS1

www.durhamcathedral.co.uk/learning/online-resources

Discover the story of St Cuthbert with downloadable resources for KS1.

Understanding Christianity

www.understandingchristianity.org.uk

This is a substantial resource to support teaching Christianity in RE from the Church of England Education Unit. The materials and resources have been developed for teachers to support pupils from EYFS to KS3 in developing their own thinking and their understanding of Christianity.

Westminster Abbey: learning resources

www.westminster-abbey.org/learning

Select Teaching Resources for a wealth of downloadable lessons, assemblies and image banks for KS1 to post-16. There is an A–Z search facility or select by subject, including: History; Politics; Religious Education; or Sociology. Excellent.

Hinduism

Hooray for Hanuman

www.dur.ac.uk/4schools/learningonline/familyactivities

Find out about Hanuman, the Hindu Monkey King. Select Hooray for Hanuman.

The story of Hanuman

www.dur.ac.uk/4schools/learningonline/secondaryonline

Discover the story of the Hindu god Hanuman.

Islam

Celebrating Eid-Al-Fitr

www.dur.ac.uk/4schools/learningonline/familyactivities

This is an activity to celebrate Eid-Al-Fitr, the Muslim festival marking the end of Ramadan. Select Celebrating Eid-Al-Fitr.

Judaism

Jewish Museum: learning resources: Judaism

www.jewishmuseum.org.uk/schools/in-the-classroom

This has extensive resources for use in the classroom or at home covering KS1 to A Level. Search by resource type, key stage or by area of study, which includes During War '39–'45; Pre-War '33–'39; Immigration and Migration; and many more. Select Curriculum, then Judaism, for a wealth of resources. Excellent.

Sikhism

Sikhism: learning resources

www.littlesikhs.com/home

A great website with lots of downloads to explain Sikhism to children along with video and worksheets to use at home or in the classroom.

Sikhism: information and timelime

www.theschoolrun.com/homework-help/sikhism

This provides facts and information about Sikhism: a timeline, images, videos, a children's booklist and links to find out more about aspects of Sikhism.

RELATIONSHIPS AND SEX

Relationships, sex, sexual health and puberty are part of the PSHE curriculum so it is important to check the resources listed under PSHE. The resources below are offered by organisations dedicated to children and young people's health and wellbeing.

Information

Anti-bullying from The Diana Award

www.antibullyingpro.com/resources

The Diana Award Anti-Bullying Campaign engages young people, parents and teachers to change the attitudes, behaviour and culture of bullying by building skills and confidence to address different situations both online and offline. The resources are fantastic, beautifully produced and simply require a request for the download. Select Diversity and Inclusion from the list of topics for a range of resources on LGBTQ+; Understanding Gender; Homophobic and Biphobic Bullying, and more. Uses videos, guides, activities, presentations and lesson plans. Excellent for either classroom or home use.

Domestic abuse: The Hide Out

www.thehideout.org.uk

This has information, advice and support for children and young people experiencing domestic abuse at home. It has online videos to support understanding of what domestic abuse is. It is very useful as a learning resource.

Friends, relationships and sex

www.childline.org.uk/info-advice/friends-relationships-sex

Excellent coverage and information for young people.

Gendered Intelligence

www.genderedintelligence.co.uk

This is packed with information and resources for young people, families and educators on understanding gender diversity. Excellent.

HIV and AIDS

www.avert.org/learn-share

Avert is an international HIV and AIDS charity based in the UK. It has excellent information for teens on Sex & Relationships; Puberty; Birth Control; Safer Sex and more. The resources can be used with upper KS3 and KS4, however they are not designed especially for young people so educators and parents should judge whether they are suitable for their intended young people.

NSPCC: sex and relationships

www.nspcc.org.uk/keeping-children-safe/sex-relationships
This provides advice and information on how to talk to young people about sex, sexuality and relationships. It covers Gender Identity; Sexuality and Sexual Orientation; Sexual Behaviour; and Healthy Relationships.

Use **https://learning.nspcc.org.uk/safeguarding-child-protection-schools** for a wealth of excellent downloadable teaching resources and lesson plans for children from 10-16 years on personal safety and healthy relationships. It covers consent, sexualised behaviour and unhealthy relationships. All resources are PSHE Association quality assured.

NSPCC: Talk Pants (the Underwear Rule)

https://learning.nspcc.org.uk/safeguarding-child-protection-schools
Select Teaching Resources, then Talk Pants. This includes lesson plans, slide presentations, curriculum links, classroom activities and supporting information.

C SCIENCE

See also: Space, astronomy and the solar system

Science is a National Curriculum subject within the four nations. There may be variations as to the way it is taught but there is no doubt that support from home can only benefit such learning. There is a wealth of materials listed below with activities to inspire and support science understanding. There are many organisations, such as the Science Museum, STEM and Jodrell Bank, who have created fun and engaging resources to use at home or at school. Some topics have been listed under the specific school of science - Biology, Chemistry or Physics. It is certainly well worth exploring the resources and having a go at some kitchen science together. This is home learning at its best and can benefit the whole family. It's fun too!

Information

National Geographic Kids: primary science resources

www.natgeokids.com/uk/teacher-category/science

This covers Animals and Insects; Dinosaurs; Evolution; Forces; Habitats; Humans; Plants; Rocks; and Space.

STEM Learning: primary science resources

www.stem.org.uk/primary-science

This includes resources on topics for Plants; Rocks; Animals including Humans; Forces & Magnets; Materials and their Properties; States of Matter; Electricity; Light; Earth & Space; Living Things; Evolution & Inheritance; and Sound. To access the resources, you are required to complete the free registration. Excellent.

Learning resources and activities

50+ STEM activities for any classroom

www.stem.org.uk

An amazing selection of activities to do at home or in the classroom. Activities are divided into Primary and Secondary with a downloadable learning resource for each, packed with activity ideas and links to full instructions and materials required. Absolutely wonderful for anyone teaching STEM or learning from home.

Aerospace Bristol: learning resources

www.aerospacebristol.org/at-home-with-aerospace-bristol

This gives lots of excellent STEM activities. It includes How to Build a Rocket Launcher and Exercise Like an Astronaut, among many others.

Association of the British Pharmaceutical Industry: science

www.abpischools.org.uk

This provides teachers, parents and young people with curriculum related, interactive resources with animations and diagrams that can be downloaded. All the resources link science topics to the world outside and particularly to the treatment of disease. Select by age range 5-7; 7-11; 11-14; 14-16; and 16+. Then further select by topic. Excellent.

Association for Science Education

www.schoolscience.co.uk

Learning and teaching resources divided by: Primary; Ages 11-14; Ages 14-16; Ages 16-18; and a Teacher Zone. For each age group there are resources by topic and within these there is a range of resources, downloads and links to partner organisations. It does require scrolling through but there are some gems to be found and it is well worth persisting.

Birmingham Museum: science learning resources

www.birminghammuseums.org.uk/school_resources

Select Science from the subject list for a host of downloadable kitchen science experiments.

Children's University: science learning activities

www.childrensuniversity.manchester.ac.uk/learning-activities/science

These resources have been developed by the Children's University in Manchester and Manchester University. The science topics covered include: The Body & Medicines; Energy and the Environment; The Earth and Beyond; Micro-organisms; and The Brain and Senses.

Jodrell Bank: science learning at home

www.jodrellbank.net/learn/sciencelearningathome

This has some themed learning resources including SETI (Search for Extra-Terrestrial Intelligence) and Aliens. Includes useful information, Aliens colouring sheets and Create Your Own Alien.

Kitchen Pantry Scientist

www.kitchenpantryscientist.com

This has lots of science experiments to do at home using kitchen ingredients.

Kitchen science booklet KS2

www.sciencemuseum.org.uk/learning

A brilliant downloadable PDF of science activities to do at home or in the classroom using everyday ingredients.

Planet Science

www.planet-science.com

This has sections for Under 11s; Over 11s; Experiments; and Parents/Teachers. It is wonderfully visual and provides a wealth of science information and resources on different science topics. It is packed with interesting material to use in the classroom or at home.

Primary school teaching ideas

www.teachingideas.co.uk/subjects/science

A huge collection of teaching ideas and resources for KS1 and KS2 Science. This has activities that cover topics such as Circuits & Electricity; Human Biology; Light; Materials; Sound; and many more. It includes activity and display posters to download for use in the classroom or at home. Excellent.

REME Museum: STEM learning resources

www.rememuseum.org.uk/family-fun

REME (Royal Electrical and Mechanical Engineer Corps) have activities and videos via REME YouTube covering STEM topics, including: DIY Light Circuit; Self-Propelled Trucks; Tracked Vehicles; Egg Box Helicopter; and Rainbow Colour Diffusion Experiment among many others. Well worth a look.

The Royal Institution: fun science to try at home

www.rigb.org/families/experimental

This has a series of short films showing how to do fun and easy science experiments at home.

Royal Mint: learning resources

www.royalmint.com/kids

Select Science for a downloadable learning resource looking at metals and how coins are made. Excellent.

Science4Families

www.seerih-innovations.org/science4families

The Science and Engineering Education Research and Innovation Hub (SEERIH) is a nationally recognised hub of science and engineering specialists. This resource, developed in conjunction with Manchester University, offers primary teachers and families activity ideas for how to learn science together in an engaging, fun and inspirational way.

STEM: future engineers activities

www.ltmuseum.co.uk/activities

London Transport Museum has a number of STEM activities to download related to engineering. Select Future Engineers Activities.

STEM Learning: A Level science

www.stem.org.uk/alevelscience

This has extensive A Level resources for Physics, Chemistry and Biology. Each topic resource identified as suitable for home learning has been highlighted as such in its title. To access the resources, you are required to complete the free registration. Excellent.

STEM Learning: secondary 11–14 science

www.stem.org.uk/secondary-science

This has extensive KS3 resources for Physics, Chemistry and Biology. Each topic resource identified as suitable for home learning has been highlighted as such in its title. To access the resources, you are required to complete the free registration. Excellent.

STEM Learning: secondary 14–16 science

www.stem.org.uk/14-16-science-resource-packages

This has extensive KS4 resources for Physics, Chemistry and Biology. Each topic resource identified as suitable for home learning has been highlighted as such in its title. To access the resources, you are required to complete the free registration. Excellent.

Winchester Science Centre and Planetarium: Science@Home

www.winchestersciencecentre.org/science-home/science-home

A fantastic and inspirational collection of resources to use at home or in the classroom. There are simple Science Sizzle experiments, hands-on activities in the Curiosity Challenges and loads of inspiration from the Indoor Science Ideas. It aims to get families learning and laughing together with activities that will enable children to build their science inquiry skills - to think creatively, design, build, test, ask questions, research and evaluate - all of which are part of STEM learning. Excellent.

Biology

Association of the British Pharmaceutical Industry: biology

www.abpischools.org.uk/age-range/14-16

Association of the British Pharmaceutical Industry: biology

www.abpischools.org.uk/age-range/16-19

These cover a wealth of topics related to biology and human biology and include: Cell Biology; Hormones; the Nervous System; Cell Division; Genes; and Infectious Diseases, plus many more.

Exploring urban nature: resources for schools

www.nhm.ac.uk/schools/teaching-resources/urban-nature-teaching-resources.html

This provides a wealth of downloadable learning resources to support curriculum-linked topics around the theme of urban nature. They include activities to support understanding of urban biodiversity and the issues affecting the local environment, including climate change and pollution. Excellent.

GEN strategy games

www.nms.ac.uk/explore-our-collections/resources/for-teachers-secondary-resources

GEN is a strategy game from the National Museum of Scotland. It uses biomedical objects from the collection to diagnose and treat a digital creature. It is designed to work on any device and is a fun way to introduce body systems, cells and diseases. Select GEN strategy game.

Life science and medicine resources

www.manchester.ac.uk/connect/teachers/teacher-events-resources/resources

These are resources designed by staff at the Faculty of Biology, Medicine and Health at Manchester University, covering a range of biology curriculum topics for primary and secondary.

Life Science Centre: science at home

www.life.org.uk/downloadable-resources

This has lots of downloadable science activities to do at home from the Life Science Centre, Newcastle. Excellent.

Living world colouring sheets

https://askabiologist.asu.edu/coloring

This has an extensive collection of colouring sheets and worksheets covering different areas of biology. Some of these would be useful for classroom learning packs and certainly for home use. The worksheets are listed alphabetically by title. Very useful.

Parasites

www.nms.ac.uk/explore-our-collections/resources/for-teachers-secondary-resources

This resource explores the challenges we face in fighting five of the most persistent parasites through games, films and articles. Suitable for BGE Science & Senior Phase Biology, GCSE and A Level. Select Parasites.

Plant and fungal science: learning resources

www.kew.org/learning/learning-at-home

Kew Gardens has a series of resources about plant and fungal science, all curriculum aligned for KS1 to KS5. They are downloadable and include videos, games and challenges. It also has an online learning platform called Endeavor, which has teaching resources for KS1 to KS5. This has videos, infographics and whiteboard presentations all free to use by registering your school to access the resource at **www.kew.org/learning/endeavour**

The Spread of Disease: Coughs and Sneezes (1945)

www.screenonline.org.uk

Select Education for access to films and television titles from 1890 to 2014. Access the Lesson Bank for links to curriculum Science. This explores the spread of disease with two comic public information films from the 1940s. It has a lesson plan for KS4 pupils using the films to understand about the spread of disease. This is very interesting and a tad too relevant in 2020/2021. Excellent.

Teeth and eating

www.childrensuniversity.manchester.ac.uk/learning-activities/science/teeth-and-eating/introduction

This is a learning resource developed by the Children's University in Manchester and the Dental Department at Manchester University. It looks at the structure of the tooth, types of teeth and the tooth timeline. Each module is a colourful set of slides with interactive questions.

Chemistry

Association of the British Pharmaceutical Industry: chemistry

www.abpischools.org.uk/age-range/16-19

Select from topics Chemistry of Life or Making Medicines for a detailed study of the basic principles and aspects of chemistry. This will also be useful to pupils studying for GCSE. Excellent.

Creative Chemistry

www.creative-chemistry.org.uk

This is a fabulous resource for chemistry students, educators and families. It covers GCSE and A Level chemistry with worksheets and practical guides on every topic. In addition, there are activity worksheets and fun stuff to do at school or at home. The chemistry crosswords and word searches are particularly useful to use at home as an alternative revision and learning tool. Excellent.

Isaac chemistry

www.isaacphysics.org/chemistry

Covers chemistry problem-solving skills for GCSE and A Level from the Education Department at Cambridge University. It is suitable for home learning. It also has a teachers site, with syllabus maps linking school content to the resources. This requires free registration, which gives teachers access to a range of teacher features.

Royal Society of Chemistry: learning resources

www.edu.rsc.org/resources

This is packed with a wealth of learning resources for primary, secondary and higher education. The Secondary section alone has over 1,000 resources. It includes teaching ideas, resources, experiments, videos and much more. It really is an inspiring learning resource. Excellent.

Periodic table

Association of the British Pharmaceutical Industry: periodic table

www.abpischools.org.uk/topic/periodic-table/1/1

This provides free information and activities on the periodic table.

Royal Society of Chemistry: periodic table

www.rsc.org/periodic-table

The Royal Society of Chemistry's interactive periodic table features history, alchemy, podcasts, videos and data trends across the periodic table.

Physics

Association of the British Pharmaceutical Industry: physics

www.abpischools.org.uk/age-range/14-16

Isaac physics

www.isaacphysics.org

This is physics learning for GCSE and A Level from the Education Department at Cambridge University. It is suitable for home learning and includes problem-solving quizzes.

National Coal Mining Museum: physics factsheets

www.ncm.org.uk/learning/learning-resources/science

This has a range of factsheets covering Light; Electricity; Forces; and Materials.

Physical sciences, engineering and maths resources

www.manchester.ac.uk/connect/teachers/teacher-events-resources/resources/fse

Here you will find science learning resources developed by the Faculty of Science and Engineering at Manchester University and education experts at the Science and Engineering Education Innovation Hub. They are designed to introduce pupils to science subjects, with primary and secondary resources available.

Topics

Forces and magnets

Royal Museums Greenwich: KS2 magnetism

www.rmg.co.uk/schools-communities/learning-resources/ks2-learning-home

Magnetism activities for KS2, including finding out about the Earth's magnetic field.

Gravity

Gravity

www.discoverymuseum.org.uk/week-11-gravity

Find out about gravity through downloadable activities.

Light

Make your own pinhole camera

www.theboxplymouth.com/schools/learning-resources/make-your-own-pinhole-camera

Suitable for KS2.

Royal Museums Greenwich: KS2 light

www.rmg.co.uk/schools-communities/learning-resources/ks2-learning-home

Light activities for KS2, including investigating how we see things.

Materials

Which everyday materials are bicycles made from and why?

www.bikeability.org.uk/tools-for-schools/learning-resources

Select KS1 to explore materials used on bicycles.

Motion and forces

Royal Museums Greenwich: KS3 Newton's Laws of Motion

www.rmg.co.uk/schools-communities/teacher-resources/newtons-laws-motion

A video with downloadable accompanying resources on Newton's Law of Motion from the Royal Observatory Greenwich.

Royal Museums Greenwich: KS4 acceleration; gravity; momentum and forces

www.rmg.co.uk/schools-communities/learning-resources/ks4-learning-home

A video and activity to find out how to calculate the acceleration due to gravity.

SPACE, ASTRONOMY AND THE SOLAR SYSTEM

Space remains a popular topic for children and young people and there is a wealth of resources to reflect such interest. As well as the learning materials below, for those wanting some interesting facts and figures the Guinness World Records **www.guinnessworldrecords.com** will not disappoint.

Information

Image Bank: Tim Peake spacecraft

https://learning.sciencemuseumgroup.org.uk/resources/image-bank-tim-peakes-spacecraft

The image bank includes photographs of Tim Peake's space journey orbiting the Earth on the International Space Station before he returned in the Soyuz TMA-19M descent module. The downloadable resources called Tim Peake Spacecraft are fabulous and will fascinate and stimulate conversation either in the classroom or at home.

Neil Armstrong

www.natgeokids.com/uk/primary-resource/neil-armstrong-primary-resource

Discover Neil Armstrong and how he became the first man on the Moon.

Learning resources and activities

The Clangers! Worksheets for EY and KS1

www.jodrellbank.net/learn/schools/resources

Worksheets include: Make a rocket with the Clangers; Have fun with the planets; and Find your way through the star maze.

Cosmic colouring-in

www.armagh.space/education/kidskorner

Space-related colouring-in sheets and crafts from Armagh Planetarium.

Doppler shift, nuclear fusion in stars, black holes and the universe

www.rmg.co.uk/schools-communities/learning-resources/ks5-learning-home

KS5 activities to understand doppler shift, nuclear fusion in stars, black holes and the universe.

Earth and space learning at home with the Royal Museums Greenwich

www.rmg.co.uk/schools-communities/learning-resources/ks2-learning-home

KS2 activities to understand and discover more about the Earth and space, including exploring moons and finding out about Mars.

Earth, moon and sun

https://education.spacecentre.co.uk/information/learning-resources

This learning resource is linked to a visit to the National Space Centre; however, the lesson plan and worksheets can be adapted for classroom or home learning on the topic and are well worth looking at.

Escape from the International Space Station

www.eo-cdt.org/escape-room/escape-room-day-1

SENSE - Centre for Satellite Data in Environmental Science provides a satellite-themed STEM activity aimed at KS2, but it could be used with children up to 16 years. Using puzzles to solve the codes, the activity covers parts of both the Science and Geography curriculum. However, it is also a great activity for any child up for a challenge on a rainy afternoon.

Moon landings: activities

www.chesterfield.gov.uk/explore-chesterfield/museum/more-from-your-museum/things-to-do/activities.aspx

Discover more about the 1976 moon landings along with activities to train to be an astronaut and to make your own rocket. Select Moon Landings.

NASA solar system exploration

https://solarsystem.nasa.gov/kids

Packed with information designed for children and young people and covering the Solar System; Planets; Moons & Asteroids; and Comets & Meteors. There is also a wealth of activities for children to do at home or at school, for example how to make your own asteroid or how to make your own nano rover.

Planet information posters

https://education.spacecentre.co.uk/information/learning-resources

Downloadable posters on each planet giving facts and figures. Excellent.

Satellites, exoplanets, dark energy and dark matter and space

www.rmg.co.uk/schools-communities/learning-resources/ks4-learning-home

KS4 activities looking at satellites, exoplanets, dark energy and dark matter and space.

Solar system learning at home with the Royal Museums Greenwich

www.rmg.co.uk/schools-communities/learning-resources

Select Early Years Foundation and KS1 from Key Stages, then Science and Astronomy from School Subjects. There are Early Years and KS1 activities to understand and discover the solar system. A wonderful set of resources that would enhance classroom learning or learning at home, while having heaps of fun.

Activities include how to make a Fruit Salad Solar System and a step-by-step guide to building a solar system in a box.

Space educational resources

www.gov.uk/government/publications/space-related-educational-resources/space-related-educational-resources

Brings together a host of space-related resources and activities for teachers and parents from a range of space organisations and other sources. It includes the European Space Education Resource Office (ESERO-UK); The National Space Academy; The European Space Agency; the UK Association of Science and Discovery Centres (ASDC); and Tim Peake's Principia Mission.

Space physics learning at home with the Royal Museums Greenwich

www.rmg.co.uk/schools-communities/learning-resources/ks3-learning-home

KS3 activities to explore space physics.

Space Place

www.spaceplace.nasa.gov

Explore earth and space with NASA. Packed with information in a clear, easily accessible format. It looks at the Earth; the Sun; the Solar System; the Universe; and Science and Technology. Each aspect is brimming with activities to try at home or at school. Within the Educators section there is an A–Z Glossary of Terms.

Space: primary school worksheets

www.jodrellbank.net/learn/schools/resources

This has downloadable resources and links on astronomy and space topics.

SPECIAL EDUCATIONAL NEEDS (SEN)

See also: PE - SEND children and PE

To offer inspirational learning for children with Special Educational Needs (SEN) requires some additional considerations and planning. The organisations listed below provide information or resources that support parents and teachers to deliver creative and suitable lessons that are tailored to needs.

Information

ACE Education

www.ace-ed.org.uk/advice-about-education-for-parents

This provides independent advice and information on state education in England for parents and carers. Select Special Education Needs for information and guides. This is an excellent starting point with clear, well-presented information and signposting.

National Association for Special Educational Needs

www.nasen.org.uk/resources

The National Association for Special Educational Needs has a series of mini guides on a range of topics for SEN. These are free to download and are useful for teachers, parents and carers.

Learning resources and activities

SEN: activities

www.holstmuseum.org.uk/learning

Select Skipping SEN for a downloadable gentle skipping activity for SEN children. Or select the Feathers Game SEN; Wallpaper SEN; or Make a Whirligig SEN. All the activities are based on Victorian childhood games.

ADHD

ADHD Foundation: information guides

www.adhdfoundation.org.uk/information/young-people

This provides downloadable information guides covering all aspects of ADHD.

Autism

National Autistic Society

www.autism.org.uk/advice-and-guidance/topics/education

This has information and advice for parents and teachers to support children with autism to learn and participate in education. It also provides links to other organisations offering resources.

Dyslexia

The Dyslexia Association

www.bdadyslexia.org.uk/advice/children

This provides information and resources for parents or carers of children with dyslexia. There is also the *Empowered Parents* pack to download on how to support dyslexic children at home and at school. In addition, it has resources for Educators on how to identify and support learners with SEN.

Music and dyslexia

www.bdadyslexia.org.uk/advice/children

Select Music and Dyslexia for information on the needs of the dyslexic child studying music.

Dyspraxia

Dyspraxia Foundation

www.dyspraxiafoundation.org.uk/about-dyspraxia/information-sheets

Dyspraxia Foundation has a long list of information sheets available to download covering early years, primary and secondary. They offer information on recognising dyspraxia and how to make adjustments for learning.

Learning disabilities

Down's Syndrome Association

www.downs-syndrome.org.uk/for-families-and-carers

This has a great set of resources for families and carers covering education, child development and health and wellbeing for early years, primary and secondary children. There are also downloads covering education.

Visual impairment

Doorway Online

www.doorwayonline.org.uk

This has a collection of free interactive and accessible educational games that are particularly suited to children with visual impairment.

Royal National Institute for the Blind: curriculum resources

www.rnib.org.uk/services-we-offer-advice-professionals-education-professionals/education-resources

This has curriculum resources to help educators meet the learning needs of children and young people with visual impairment. The classroom resources are excellent for teachers, educators and parents.

Sight Advice: resources and activities

www.sightadvicefaq.org.uk/coronavirus-information/CYPF/cv-extracirc
Includes links for activities to do with children with visual impairment.

VICTA Parent Portal: education online resources

www.victaparents.org.uk/resources/education/online-resources
VICTA Parent Portal is for families with a child either blind or partially-sighted and provides links to learning resources for children and young people with visual impairment.

WEIGHTS AND MEASURES

Information

Online conversion

www.onlineconversion.com

This converts anything to anything else! It has thousands of units and millions of conversions. Not only fascinating but also very impressive.

Learning resources and activities

Weights and measures

www.teachingideas.co.uk/subjects/measure

KS1 and KS2 teaching resources and ideas on the theme of Weights and Measures. It has downloadable activity sheets that can be used in the classroom or at home. Excellent.

Index